Englisch: Kurzgeschichten Lefür Anfänger und Fortgeschrittene (mit Audioaufnahmen)

VERBESSERN SIE IHRE ENGLISCHEN LESE UND SCHREIBKENNTNISSE

Jack Cactus

Vorwort

Ich wette, du liebst Geschichten. Jeder tut es. Tatsächlich erzählen sich Menschen seit Anbeginn der Zeit welche. Von Geschichten, die beim flackerndem Feuer oder unter der Nachttischlampe erzählt wurden - Geschichten waren schon immer ein großer Teil in unserem täglichen Leben und werden es auch immer bleiben.

Aber wusstest du auch, dass die Kraft der Geschichten helfen kann, effektiv eine neue Sprache zu lernen? Mit dem richtigen Werkzeug und Methoden, können dir Geschichten sowohl dabei helfen, eine weite Vielfalt an neuen Vokabeln zu lernen, als auch deine Lese- und Hörfähigkeiten zu verbessern.

Aus genau diesem Grund, bin ich sehr froh mit Dir dieses neue Buch teilen zu dürfen. Mit sieben (7) verschiedenen Kurzgeschichten über einen Strandbesuch, Partnersuche, Feiertage, Einkaufen, Haustiere, Essen/ Kochen und Pflanzen/ Gartenarbeit, wirst du Englisch lernen, während du die Geschichten genießt.

Was kannst du von diesem Buch erwarten?

- **Zeit, das Wörterbuch wegzustecken.** Das Buch hat ein eigenes integriertes Wörterbuch in jeder Geschichte. Darum brauchst du keine Wörter nachzuschlagen, die du nicht verstehst. Dies vereinfacht den Lernprozess.

- **Lerne eine vielfältige Reihe an Vokabeln und Grammatikstrukturen.** Die Geschichten sind mit einem weiten Spektrum an hilfreichen Wörtern und Grammatik geschrieben, die du gut im alltäglichen Leben gebrauchen kannst.

- **Verbessere dein Leseverständnis und deine Schreibfähigkeiten.** Geführt bei den einfachen Geschichten und den zugehörigen Schreibübungen, wirst du gefragt, deine eigene Zusammenfassung mit deinen eigenen Worten zu schreiben.

- **Verstärke deine Hörfähigkeiten und Aussprache in Englisch.** Mithilfe des Hörbuchs kannst du dir die Geschichten aus der Sicht eines Muttersprachlers anhören. Das Hörbuch hat zwei Versionen: Erzählung in normaler Geschwindigkeit für fortgeschrittene Anfänger und eine langsame Geschwindigkeit für Anfänger. So kannst du gut mitkommen und deine Aussprache üben.

Ich hoffe, du hast genauso viel Spaß das Buch zu lesen wie ich ihn hatte es zu schreiben. Aber am wichtigsten: Ich hoffe, dass es dir dabei hilft, deine Ziele in der englischen Sprache zu erreichen!

Viel Glück und viel Vergnügen!

Jack Cactus

Table of Contents

A trip to the Beach

Anleitung zur Nutzung der Audio-Datei

Marie loved the **beach**. It was her **favorite place** in the **entire world**. It didn't matter which beach it was. She had visited many beaches in many places and she loved them all. What **mattered** to her was the **sand between** her **toes**, the **sound** of the **waves crashing**, and the **wind blowing** in her hair. Most of the time, thinking of the beach made her **heart** feel at **peace**, and it always made her smile.

beach - Strand
favorite place – Lieblingsort
entire world – ganze Welt
mattered - bedeutete
sand between – Sand zwischen
toes - Zehen
sound – Geräusch/Klang
waves crashing – Zusammenstoß der Wellen
wind blowing – Wind weht
heart - Herz
peace - Frieden

Now Marie has two young **children**, and she is **pregnant** with a third, which makes going to the beach much more **difficult** than it used to be. She used to just **hop in the car** and go **whenever** she **pleased**, but now it was **not so easy**! She still loved to be at the beach, but now she had to **consider** the kids' **schedules**, along with her own and her **husband's**, just to plan the trip. Then Marie and her husband had to get the kids **ready to go**, get **themselves** ready to go, and get everyone's **luggage packed**. Then they had to **drive** to the beach and the **closest** one was four **hours** away! Marie felt **exhausted** just thinking about it.

A trip to the Beach

children - Kinder
pregnant - Schwanger
difficult - schwierig
hop in the car (exp) – hüpfte ins Auto
whenever – Wann immer
pleased - gefallen
not so easy (exp) – nicht so einfach
consider - beachten
schedules – Pläne
husband›s - Ehemann
ready to go (exp) – bereitmachen
themselves – sich selbst
luggage packed – Koffer gepackt
drive - fahren
closest – am nächsten
hours - Stunden
exhausted - erschöpft

Spring break was coming up, and the kids would be **off** school for a week. She and her husband, John, decided that they would plan a trip to the beach and stay in a **hotel** for a **couple** of days. They had not been on **vacation** in **years**, and they needed to **relax**.

spring break - Frühlingsferien
off – frei
hotel – Hotel/ Pension
couple - Paar
vacation - Urlaub
years - Jahre
relax - entspannen

"We're going to the beach for your spring break," John told the children.

"Yay!" the children cried.

"I want to build a great big **sandcastle**," said Trevor, the **eldest**, who was eight **years old**.

“I want to find a white **seashell**,” said Kitty, the **youngest**, who was **five years old**.

“I want to drink a **cocktail** on the **balcony**,” John said under his breath. Marie **playfully slapped** his arm and **reminded** him that he **shouldn’t** say such things around the kids.

“I want to get a nice **tan**,” Marie **sighed**.

sandcastle - Sandburg
eldest - älteste
years old – Jahre alt
seashell - Muschel
youngest - jüngster
five years old – fünf Jahre alt
cocktail – Cocktail (Mixgetränk)
balcony - Balkon
playfully slapped – schlug ihn neckisch
reminded - erinnert
shouldn’t – sollte nicht
tan – braungebrannte Haut
sighed - seufzte

They waited and waited, making plans and talking about how excited they were about **going on vacation** to the beach. They were staying for five whole days. It would be **expensive** for Marie and John because the hotel was not cheap, but they knew it would be **worth it**.

going on vacation (exp) – in den Urlaub gehen
expensive - teuer
worth it (exp) – war es wert

Spring break finally **arrived**. Marie **woke the children up** very early in the morning while it was still dark. She helped them get their **suitcases** and luggage into the car while John **loaded** hers and his own. Then, they started on the long drive to the beach.

A trip to the Beach

arrived - angekommen
woke the children up (exp) – Kinder aufgeweckt
suitcases - Koffer
loaded - beladen

For the first hour the kids **slept**, Marie **dozed**, and John **drove**. It was still dark. The sky turned pale blue, then pale pink, then **brilliant** pink and orange as the sun **rose**. They stopped at a little **cafe** to get some breakfast and coffee. The kids ate **pancakes**, Marie had **oatmeal** and fruit, and John had an **omelet**. John and Marie got some coffee to go, then they **piled** back in the car and kept driving.

slept - schliefen
dozed - schlummerte
drove - gefahren
brilliant -glänzend
rose - aufstieg
cafe - Café
pancakes - Pfannkuchen
oatmeal - Haferbrei
omelet - Omelett
piled -gehäuft

"Mama, I'm ***bored,*** " **whined** Trevor.

"Count all the red cars," **suggested** Marie.

"Mama, I'm bored too," said Kitty.

"Count all the white cars," suggested Marie.

"Mama, I'm bored *too,*" John **teased**.

"Count all the miles between here and the beach," Marie **laughed**.

bored - gelangweilt
whined -wimmerte

suggested -vorschlagen
teased - stichelte
laughed - lachte

As they drove, Marie thought about their third child, who was **due** to be **born** in a few **weeks**. She and John did not want to know **whether** the baby was a boy or a girl until the baby was born, so Marie had **come up with** many names she **liked**. She **wondered** if Trevor and Kitty would **get along** with the new baby. She wondered if she would ever **fit** into her old **blue jeans** again. She wondered if the child would like **sports** or if they would **prefer indoor** activities like **reading**. Kitty was an **outdoor** girl, while Trevor liked both but preferred things like **video games** and **cooking** with Mama. She wondered if John ever **minded** that she was a **stay-at-home mom**. Was he ever **resentful** that she quit her job to **raise the kids**? He always seemed **grateful** when he came home to a **clean** house full of happy children and a good **home-cooked** meal, so Marie tried not to **worry** too much.

due - fällig
born - geboren
weeks - Wochen
whether - ob
come up with (exp) – sich etwas ausdenken
liked - gefielen
wondered - wunderte
get along (exp) – sich verstehen
fit - passen
blue jeans – blaue Jeans
sports - Sport
prefer indoor – Innen bevorzugen
reading - Lesen
outdoor - Im Freien
video games – Videospiele
cooking - kochen
minded - beachtet
stay-at-home mom - Heimische Mutter
resentful - übel nehmen

raise the kids (exp) – Kinder erziehen
grateful - dankbar
clean - sauber
home-cooked – hausgemacht
worry – sorgen machen

“How many red cars have you **counted**?” Marie asked after a while.

“Eleventy-twelve,” Trevor said **confidently**.

“Even I know that’s not a real **number**!” **cried** Kitty. “I counted five.”

“There were more than five,” Trevor **insisted**. “You’re just saying that ‘cause you’re five years old.”

counted - gezählt
confidently - selbstbewusst
number - Nummer
cried - geweint
insisted – bestand darauf

“Am not,” Kitty **protested**, but **secretly** it was true. Five was her favorite number.

“Children, don’t **fight**, please,” Marie **admonished**. She could feel a **headache** coming on, and they still had a long way to ride. She **fished** in her bag for a couple of **action figures** and handed them to Kitty in the back seat. “Why don’t you play with those? Give one to Trevor.”

protested - protestierte
secretly - heimlich
fight - streiten
admonished - ermahnte
headache - Kopfschmerzen

fished - griff
action figures – Actionfiguren

The action figures kept the children **occupied** for a long time. They fell asleep again after that, and it was **lunchtime** when they arrived at the beach. **Check-in** at the **hotel** was not until 3:00PM, so they went to a **sea food restaurant** to eat lunch together. Marie ordered **shrimp scampi, hoping** it would not **upset her stomach**. The kids wanted **fish sticks** and **french fries**, while John **opted** for **surf** and **turf**.

occupied - beschäftigte
lunchtime - Mittagessenszeit
Check-in - einchecken
hotel - Hotel
seafood restaurant – Restaurant für Meeresfrüchte
shrimp scampi - Schrimps
hoping - gehofft
upset her stomach (exp) – bereitet ihr Magenschmerzen
fishsticks - Fischstäbchen
french fries - Pommes
opted - entschied
surf - surfen
turf – Torf (surf ´n´ turf = Hauptgericht in Steakhäusern)

Finally, it was time to check in to the hotel. The hotel **lobby** was **spacious** and **airy** with many **potted plants** and lots of **sunshine**. The weather was **mild** and all the windows were open. The lady at the desk smiled a lot. She had dark brown hair **pulled** into a **tight bun** at the back of her head and she wore bright red **lipstick**. Then they took their luggage to the room, which looked out over the **oceanfront**, and changed their clothes. There was still time to go to the beach!

Finally - endlich
lobby - Empfangsbereich
spacious - geräumig

airy - luftig
potted plants – Topfpflanzen
sunshine - Sonnenschein
mild - sanft
pulled -gebunden
tight bun – enger Zopf
lipstick - Lippenstift
oceanfront - Meeresblick

"Wait, children, you need to put on **sunscreen**," Marie said as Trevor and Kitty ran for the door. "You don't want to get **sunburned**! John, you help Trevor and I'll help Kitty." Marie took her daughter's hand and began **applying** sunscreen to her hands, **instructing** her where and how to rub it in.

No one wanted to be at the beach more than Marie, but by the time the children were ready to go to the water she was **exhausted**!

sunscreen - Sonnencreme
sunburned - Sonnenbrand
applying - auftragen
instructing - anweisen
exhausted - erschöpft

"John, you all **go ahead**. I'm going to lay down for a while. I will **catch up with you** later."

Once everyone was gone, Marie sat on the edge of the bed in her pink bikini patting her tummy. She was excited for their third child, but this baby was **wearing her out**! She felt tired often these days. Her feet hurt, it was hard to eat because her **appetite** was **irregular**, and sometimes it was even hard to walk! She would be glad when this baby decided it was time to come out. For now, she would have to be **content** with taking a nap before she could enjoy the beach. Marie laid down and fell asleep almost **immediately**.

go ahead – vorausgehen
catch up with you - aufholen
wearing her out – leierte sie aus
appetite - Appetit
irregular - unregelmäßig
content - zufrieden
immediately - sofort

She woke an hour later, sat up with a little bit of a **struggle** and **stretched**. The sun was still out! She struggled to get to her feet too, but **she made it**. Marie looked at herself in the **full-length mirror** in the bathroom and smiled. Some women did not like how they looked while **carrying** a **child**, but Marie thought she looked perfect. She put her hair in a **ponytail** and made her way down to the beach.

struggle – Anstrengung
stretched - strecken
she made it (exp) – sie hat es geschafft
full-length – voller länge
mirror - Spiegel
carrying - tragen
child - Kind
ponytail - Pferdeschwanz

John had **rented** an **umbrella** and the kids were playing with some new friends. Trevor was **keen** on making the best sandcastle on the beach and the other children had special **buckets** for making sandcastle shapes. Kitty was helping because she liked to do whatever Trevor was doing. John was sitting under the umbrella and watching the children, but when he saw Marie coming he stood up and took her hand and **kissed her hello**.

rented - ausgeliehen
umbrella - Regenschirm
buckets - Eimer
keen – eifrig / begeistert
kissed her hello (exp) – gab ihr einen Begrüßungskuss

A trip to the Beach

"How was your nap?" he asked.

"Really nice," she **panted**, out of breath from the short walk down to the beach. "I'll be happy to have **energy** again once the baby is born!"

Marie walked the rest of the way down the sand to the water. She **in haled deeply**, **relishing** the **sweet**, **salty breeze whipping** her **curly** black hair around, and the **tangy** smell of **coconut tanning oil** someone was using nearby. She **curled** her toes in the wet sand and closed her eyes to listen to the **waves crashing**. Right as a wave **broke** and **washed** over her feet she felt the baby **kick**, her eyes opened and she laughed, **pressing** her **palm** to the spot on her tummy. Even though she was tired, Marie felt content as she stood with her feet in the **surf**, looking at the sunset, and **hearing** the waves crash and her children laughing **behind** her.

panted - keuchte
energy - Energie
inhaled deeply – tief eingeatmet
relishing - genießen
sweet - süß
salty breeze whipping – salzige Luftbrise
curly - lockig
tangy - streng
coconut tanning oil – Kokos-Bräunungsöl
curled - kringelte
waves crashing – Wellen aufschlagen
washed - floss
broke – zusammenbrach
kick - Tritt
pressing - drückte
palm - Handfläche
surf - Brandung
hearing - hören
behind - hinter

They came back to the beach right after **breakfast** the next day. Everyone put on lots of **sun block** and Marie took a little nap under their umbrella while John played **Frisbee** with the kids. They ate lunch on the beach: **peanut butter sandwiches**, cold water and cold **apples** from a **cooler** full of **ice**. Marie went **swimming** with Trevor, but Kitty **wasn›t allowed** yet because she was too small. Kitty cried until John started **hunting** for seashells with her and then she **forgot** all about swimming. Marie and Trevor swam past the **breakers**, where it was easy to just **float** on the **waves** like a **seagull**. Trevor started a **splash fight**, which Marie won because she was the **queen** of splash fights!

breakfast - Frühstück
sunblock - Sonnenblocker
Frisbee – Frisbee (Wurfscheibe)
peanut butter sandwiches – Erdnussbutter Brot
apples - Äpfel
cooler - Kühlbox
ice - Eis
swimming - schwimmen
wasn›t allowed – nicht erlaubt
hunting - jagen
forgot - vergessen
breakers - Brandung
float - gleiten
waves - Wellen
seagull - Seemöwe
splash fight – Platschkampf
queen - Königin

After another sandwich and some rest, the whole family decided to go for a walk on the beach. Marie walked arm-in-arm with John as the kids ran ahead, **shrieking** and **splashing** each other and **throwing fistfuls** of **sand** until John told them to **cut it out**.

shrieking - kreischend
splashing - anspritzen

throwing fistfuls – Handvoll werfen
sand - Sand
cut it out - aufhören

About twenty **minutes** in to the walk, Marie's **stomach** started to feel **strange**. It felt **tight** and it was **painful**! She **stopped walking** and **grabbed** John's hand. "I think the baby is coming!" she **gasped**.

"Kids, follow me!" John said. He **easily lifted** Marie in his arms and began **carrying** her up the beach. "My wife is **having a baby**!" he **announced** to no one in **particular**.

minutes - Minuten
stomach - Magen
strange - komisch
tight - eng
painful - schmerzhaft
stopped walking – aufgehört zu laufen
grabbed - fasste
gasped - keuchte
easily lifted – mühelos gehoben
carrying - tragen
having a baby – ein Baby bekommen (gebären)
announced - angekündigt
particular - speziell

"Our little sister is coming!" cried Kitty.

"Our little brother is coming!" cried Trevor.

"Can someone help us? We're about a **mile** away from our car! I have to get my wife to a **hospital**!" John cried.

"I'm **parked** close by, let me give you a **ride**," **offered** an older **gentleman** wearing a **colorful Hawaiian shirt**.

John **considered** him, then considered his wife, then **nodded**. "All right, thank you, yes, we'd **be much obliged**," he said. "Come on, children."

"Daddy we're not supposed to talk to **strangers**," Trevor **reminded** John **dutifully**. "And never, *ever* get in a stranger's car!"

mile - Meile
hospital - Krankenhaus
parked - geparkt
colorful Hawaiian shirt – buntes hawaiianisches Oberteil
considered - ansehen, berücksichtigen
nodded - nickte
be much obliged (exp) – sehr dankbar
strangers - Fremde
reminded - erinnert
dutifully - pflichtbewusst

"That's right," Kitty **piped up**.

"You're right, kids, this is a very **unusual decision**," John **agreed**. "But it's okay because Mommy and I are both here. It'll be okay. Just never do it **by yourselves**, okay?"

"Is Mommy going to have the baby in the car?" Kitty wondered **aloud**.

"**Probably** not," the man in the colorful shirt said to her. "What's your name, kid?"

"... Kitty," she said **shyly**.

piped up - piepste
unusual decision – ungewöhnliche Entscheidung
agreed - zustimmen
by yourselves - alleine
aloud - laut

Probably - wahrscheinlich
shyly - schüchtern

"Hiya Kitty, you can call me Charlie. And what's your name, **fella**?" he said to Trevor.

"Trevor," he said **sullenly**. "Why are you driving us to the hospital?"

"Well, my own wife was in a **similar situation**," Charlie explained. "We were on this very same beach in fact, over thirty years ago, when she started having our first child!"

"Was it a boy or a girl?" Kitty wanted to know.

"A boy," Charlie said. "We named him Samuel, but everyone calls him Sammy to this day."

They reached Charlie's car, which was an old green **station wagon**. John and Marie and Kitty got in the **backseat** while Trevor got **to ride shotgun**.

"Charlie, hurry!" John **urged**.

"I'm hurrying!" Charlie cried. "There's a lot of **traffic** today. **Darn tourists**..."

"Hey! *We're* tourists," Trevor reminded him.

Fella - Kumpel
sullenly - mürrisch
similar situation – ähnliche Situation
station wagon – Kombiwagen
backseat - Rücksitz
to ride shotgun (exp) – Beifahrer sein
urged -drängte
traffic - Verkehr
Darn tourists – verdammte Touristen

Marie was **clinging** tightly to John the whole time. When they got to the hospital, she was in a lot of pain and could not walk at all. They rushed her in and John followed while Trevor and Kitty waited with Charlie. Charlie didn't mind waiting and **keeping an eye on** the kids. There were some **puzzles** and little **toys** for kids in the waiting room which kept Trevor and Kitty **occupied** for a while, but everyone was very excited about the new baby. Trevor kept running across the waiting room and asking the **nurse** if they could see their baby brother yet.

clinging - festhalten
keeping an eye on (exp) – im Auge behalten
puzzles - Puzzle
toys - Spielzeug
occupied - beschäftigt
nurse - Krankenschwester

"Or sister!" Kitty **added** every time.

It took a long, long time. Charlie got some snacks from the cafeteria because it was dinner time, and Trevor and Kitty got a kick out of eating chips and candy bars for dinner. The kids fell asleep not long after that, because it had been a long, exciting day!

Around **midnight**, the nurse woke them up and she led Charlie, Trevor, and Kitty through the hospital to the room where their mom was staying.

Marie looked very **pale** and very **tired**, but she could not stop smiling. The baby was in her arms, **swaddled** in a soft white **blanket**. "Children, come meet your new baby brother," Marie told them.

added - hinzufügen
midnight - Mitternacht
pale - blass
tired - müde

swaddled - eingewickelt
blanket - Decke

"I told you!" Trevor cried **triumphantly**. Kitty did not seem **disappointed** as she **scurried** over and **hopped** up on the bed beside her mother to look **curiously** at the red-faced **infant**.

"He's so **cute**," Kitty **cooed**.

"I'm going to teach him how to play video games," said Trevor.

"Charlie, I can't thank you enough for all your help today," said John. The men **shook hands**.

"It was my **pleasure**. You have a **lovely family**, John. I enjoyed my time with the kids! Reminds me of when I had **little ones** of my own."

"What's his name?" Kitty asked.

"His name is Charlie," Marie said with a grin.

"You're **teasing** me!" Charlie exclaimed.

"Not at all," Marie **answered**. "John wanted to call him Ernest if he was a boy, but I thought Charlie was a much better **fit**."

"That's mighty **sweet of you**, ma'am," Charlie said **bashfully**.

"If it weren't for you, Charlie might have been born in the sand!" John laughed. "In fact, we're calling his **middle name** Beach. Charlie Beach."

"That's a **silly** name," Kitty **observed**.

"Kitty is a silly name," Trevor observed.

"Oh, children," Marie sighed with a smile.

triumphantly - triumphierend
disappointed - enttäuscht
scurried - huschte
hopped - hüpfte
curiously - neugierig
infant - Kleinkind
cute - süß
cooed -gurrte
shook hands – Hände schütteln
pleasure - Vergnügen
lovely family – liebevolle Familie
little ones (exp) – Kleine Kinder
teasing - ärgern
answered - antwortete
fit - passender
sweet of you (exp) – wie lieb von dir
bashfully - verlegen
middle name – zweiter Vorname
silly - alberner
observed - beobachtete

Vocabulary:

beach - Strand
favorite place – Lieblingsort
entire world – ganze Welt
mattered - bedeutete
sand between – Sand zwischen
toes - Zehen
sound – Geräusch/Klang
waves crashing – Zusammenstoß der Wellen
wind blowing – Wind weht
heart - Herz
peace - Frieden
children - Kinder
pregnant - Schwanger
difficult - schwierig
hop in the car (exp) – hüpfte ins Auto
whenever – Wann immer
pleased - gefallen
not so easy (exp) – nicht so einfach
consider - beachten
schedules – Pläne
husband›s - Ehemann
ready to go (exp) – bereitmachen
themselves – sich selbst
luggage packed – Koffer gepackt
drive - fahren
closest – am nächsten
hours - Stunden
exhausted - erschöpft
spring break - Frühlingsferien
off – frei
hotel – Hotel/ Pension
couple - Paar
vacation - Urlaub
years - Jahre
relax - entspannen

sandcastle - Sandburg
eldest - älteste
years old – Jahre alt
seashell - Muschel
youngest - jüngster
five years old – fünf Jahre alt
cocktail – Cocktail (Mixgetränk)
balcony - Balkon
playfully slapped – schlug ihn neckisch
reminded - erinnert
shouldn›t – sollte nicht
tan – braungebrannte Haut
sighed - seufzte
going on vacation (exp) – in den Urlaub gehen
expensive - teuer
worth it (exp) – war es wert
arrived - angekommen
woke the children up (exp) – Kinder aufgeweckt
suitcases - Koffer
loaded - beladen
slept - schliefen
dozed - schlummerte
drove - gefahren
brilliant -glänzend
rose - aufstieg
cafe - Café
pancakes - Pfannkuchen
oatmeal - Haferbrei
omelet - Omelett
piled -gehäuft
bored - gelangweilt
whined -wimmerte
suggested -vorschlagen
teased - stichelte
laughed - lachte
due - fällig
born - geboren
weeks - Wochen

whether - ob
come up with (exp) – sich etwas ausdenken
liked - gefielen
wondered - wunderte
get along (exp) – sich verstehen
fit - passen
blue jeans – blaue Jeans
sports - Sport
prefer indoor – Innen bevorzugen
reading - Lesen
outdoor - Im Freien
video games – Videospiele
cooking - kochen
minded - beachtet
stay-at-home mom - Heimische Mutter
resentful - übel nehmen
raise the kids (exp) – Kinder erziehen
grateful - dankbar
clean - sauber
home-cooked – hausgemacht
worry – sorgen machen
counted - gezählt
confidently - selbstbewusst
number - Nummer
cried - geweint
insisted – bestand darauf
protested - protestierte
secretly - heimlich
fight - streiten
admonished - ermahnte
headache - Kopfschmerzen
fished - griff
action figures – Actionfiguren
occupied - beschäftigte
lunchtime - Mittagessenszeit
Check-in - einchecken
hotel - Hotel
seafood restaurant – Restaurant für Meeresfrüchte

shrimp scampi - Schrimps
hoping - gehofft
upset her stomach (exp) – bereitet ihr Magenschmerzen
fishsticks - Fischstäbchen
french fries - Pommes
opted - entschied
surf - surfen
turf – Torf (surf ´n´ turf = Hauptgericht in Steakhäusern)
Finally - endlich
lobby - Empfangsbereich
spacious - geräumig
airy - luftig
potted plants – Topfpflanzen
sunshine - Sonnenschein
mild - sanft
pulled -gebunden
tight bun – enger Zopf
lipstick - Lippenstift
oceanfront - Meeresblick
sunscreen - Sonnencreme
sunburned - Sonnenbrand
applying - auftragen
instructing - anweisen
exhausted - erschöpft
go ahead – vorausgehen
catch up with you - aufholen
wearing her out – leierte sie aus
appetite - Appetit
irregular - unregelmäßig
content - zufrieden
immediately - sofort
struggle – Anstrengung
stretched - strecken
she made it (exp) – sie hat es geschafft
full-length – voller länge
mirror - Spiegel
carrying - tragen
child - Kind

A trip to the Beach

ponytail - Pferdeschwanz
rented - ausgeliehen
umbrella - Regenschirm
buckets - Eimer
keen – eifrig / begeistert
kissed her hello (exp) – gab ihr einen Begrüßungskuss
panted - keuchte
energy - Energie
inhaled deeply – tief eingeatmet
relishing - genießen
sweet - süß
salty breeze whipping – salzige Luftbrise
curly - lockig
tangy - streng
coconut tanning oil – Kokos-Bräunungsöl
curled - kringelte
waves crashing – Wellen aufschlagen
washed - floss
broke – zusammenbrach
kick - Tritt
pressing - drückte
palm - Handfläche
surf - Brandung
hearing - hören
behind - hinter
breakfast - Frühstück
sunblock - Sonnenblocker
Frisbee – Frisbee (Wurfscheibe)
peanut butter sandwiches – Erdnussbutter Brot
apples - Äpfel
cooler - Kühlbox
ice - Eis
swimming - schwimmen
wasn›t allowed – nicht erlaubt
hunting - jagen
forgot - vergessen

breakers - Brandung
float - gleiten
waves - Wellen
seagull - Seemöwe
splash fight – Platschkampf
queen - Königin
shrieking - kreischend
splashing - anspritzen
throwing fistfuls – Handvoll werfen
sand - Sand
cut it out - aufhören
minutes - Minuten
stomach - Magen
strange - komisch
tight - eng
painful - schmerzhaft
stopped walking – aufgehört zu laufen
grabbed - fasste
gasped - keuchte
easily lifted – mühelos gehoben
carrying - tragen
having a baby – ein Baby bekommen (gebären)
announced - angekündigt
particular - speziell
mile - Meile
hospital - Krankenhaus
parked - geparkt
colorful Hawaiian shirt – buntes hawaiianisches Oberteil
considered - ansehen, berücksichtigen
nodded - nickte
be much obliged (exp) – sehr dankbar
strangers - Fremde
reminded - erinnert
dutifully - pflichtbewusst
piped up - piepste
unusual decision – ungewöhnliche Entscheidung

agreed - zustimmen
by yourselves - alleine
aloud - laut
Probably - wahrscheinlich
shyly - schüchtern
Fella - Kumpel
sullenly - mürrisch
similar situation – ähnliche Situation
station wagon – Kombiwagen
backseat - Rücksitz
to ride shotgun (exp) – Beifahrer sein
urged -drängte
traffic - Verkehr
Darn tourists – verdammte Touristen
clinging - festhalten
keeping an eye on (exp) – im Auge behalten
puzzles - Puzzle
toys - Spielzeug
occupied - beschäftigt
nurse - Krankenschwester
added - hinzufügen
midnight - Mitternacht
pale - blass
tired - müde
swaddled - eingewickelt
blanket - Decke
triumphantly - triumphierend
disappointed - enttäuscht
scurried - huschte
hopped - hüpfte
curiously - neugierig
infant - Kleinkind
cute - süß
cooed -gurrte
shook hands – Hände schütteln

pleasure - Vergnügen
lovely family – liebevolle Familie
little ones (exp) – Kleine Kinder
teasing - ärgern
answered - antwortete
fit - passender
sweet of you (exp) – wie lieb von dir
bashfully - verlegen
middle name – zweiter Vorname
silly - alberner
observed - beobachtete

Best Birthday Ever

Raquel woke up the morning of her twentieth birthday feeling **like a million bucks**.

She got out of bed as soon as her alarm **went off**. Usually, Raquel was not a morning person and she felt tired until her first cup of coffee of the day, but the morning of her twentieth birthday, she felt **amazing**! She got up and **stretched** with a big **yawn** and went into the bathroom to get ready for class.

like a million bucks (exp) – wie ne´ Millionen Dollar zu haben (Redewendung)
Went off – ging aus
morning person (exp) – Morgenmüffel
amazing - erstaunlich
stretched - streckte
yawn - gähnen

"Wow," said Raquel as she looked in the mirror. She was having a **good hair day**. She had long, thick, dark brown hair that usually had a **mind of its own**. This morning, her hair already looked almost perfect. She brushed her hair with her favorite **baby blue** hairbrush until it was smooth and shiny, then she pulled it back into a **bouncy ponytail** on the top of her head. Because it was her birthday, Raquel was feeling **fancy**, so she decided to put on some **makeup** too. First, she **applied** black **eyeliner** and made sure that the lines were winged like she saw in **fashion magazines**. Then she put on some black **mascara**, which made her **eyelashes** look thick and long. Then she put on some bright red **lipstick**, which was **fashionable** and **festive**. To top it all off, Raquel splashed on some of her favorite perfume; it was expensive, over a hundred dollars a bottle, but it made her smell like a movie star.

good hair day (exp) – Gute-Frisur-Tag
mind of its own (exp) – eigenwillig war
baby blue – Babyblau
bouncy ponytail – lockerer Pferdeschwanz
fancy - schick
makeup - Schminke
applied - auftragen
eyeliner - Eyeliner
fashion magazines – Mode-Zeitschriften
mascara - Wimperntusche
eyelashes - Wimpern
lipstick - Lippenstift
fashionable - modisch
festive - festlich

Next, Raquel went to get dressed. She chose a bright red **blouse** that matched her lipstick, a black **ballerina skirt** and cute black **flats**. She admired herself in the mirror, thinking that she was the most beautiful girl on campus. And why shouldn't she be? It was her birthday!

blouse - Bluse
ballerina skirt – Ballerina Rock
flats – Ballerinas (Schuhart, meist getragen beim Ballett)

Raquel went to the **kitchenette** in her dorm room and started **brewing** a cup of coffee. She loved coffee. Dark roast was her favorite and once she had a nice strong cup brewed, she put lots of cream and sugar in it. Usually, Raquel liked to eat a very healthy breakfast with yogurt and some fresh fruit, but she decided, because it was her birthday, that she could **indulge** in her favorite breakfast **pastry**: a **Boston cream doughnut**. The only problem was, Raquel didn't have any Boston cream doughnuts at home so she had to stop at the campus coffee shop to buy one.

kitchenette - Kochniesche
brewing - kochte

indulge -verwöhnen
pastry - Gebäck
Boston cream doughnut – Boston Crème Donut

She approached the counter at the coffee shop and smiled brightly. The cashier was a very cute boy that Raquel recognized from one of her classes. He smiled back at her and he was so **handsome** when he smiled that Raquel forgot to order.

"Can I help you?" the boy asked. Raquel looked at his name tag. His name was Michael.

"Oh! Yes, I want a Boston cream doughnut, please." She pointed at the one she wanted sitting in the glass case.

Michael took out the doughnut using a little piece of waxed paper and put it in a doughnut-sized paper bag. He handed it across the counter to Raquel, still smiling. **Boy**, was he handsome when he smiled!

"Thanks," said Raquel, "how much do I owe you?"

"You don't owe me anything, we're having a special **promotion** today," Michael said. "Pretty girls get one Boston cream doughnut for free."

Raquel **erupted** in a fit of **giggles** and **blushed**, hiding her face behind the paper bag containing the doughnut. "It's perfect!" she **exclaimed**.

"What is?" Michael asked.

"Today is my birthday," Raquel explained **shyly**, "so it's like a birthday present!"

"Happy birthday!" Michael exclaimed. "Do you have any big plans for celebrating your birthday?"

"I don't know," Raquel admitted, "I have classes all day, but I was going to ask my friends to go to dinner later." She paused, then **beamed** at Michael. "Do you want to come to dinner?"

"That would be **awesome**," said Michael, still smiling his **ridiculously** handsome smile.

"Can I get your number?" asked Raquel. She handed her phone across the counter and let Michael type in his cell phone number and name. He handed the phone back to her and she thanked him. "I'll **text** you later! I'm finished with class around four."

"Great! I get off at four. **See you later**."

"Bye!"

handsome – gutaussehend (Mann)
Boy (exp) - Mensch
promotion - Aktion
erupted - ausbrechen
giggles - kichern
blushed – erröten
exclaimed - ausgerufen
shyly - schüchtern
beamed - strahlte
awesome - wundervoll
ridiculously - lächerlich
text - schreibe
See you later (exp) – Bis Später

Michael watched the girl walk away, **admiring** her legs and her puffy black skirt. He felt a little bit **dizzy** because the girl was so beautiful, and friendly, and she smelled nice, and Michael had decided that she was pretty much perfect. He could **hardly believe** that she invited him to dinner on her birthday! He was practically a **stranger**.

admiring - bewundern
dizzy - schwindelig
hardly believe (exp) – nicht glauben können
stranger - Fremder

The rest of Michael's **shift** at the coffee shop went by very, very slowly. He kept thinking about how red the girl's lips looked, and how white her teeth were, and how brown her hair was. He got **butterflies in his stomach** when he remembered her giggling when he **flirted** with her.

shift - Schicht
butterflies in his stomach (exp) – Schmetterlinge im Bauch
flirted - geflirtet

Time slowed to a crawl. Michael was very distracted while he worked. He was usually a very good employee, but today, he got orders wrong, **burned** the milk while making a **latte**, and even **accidentally** ignored a customer while **staring into space** and thinking about the girl! The customer **berated** him and his manager **scolded** him, but Michael didn't care because he had a date tonight with the most perfect girl in the world.

Time slowed to a crawl (exp) – die Zeit blieb fast stehen
burned - verbrannt
latte – Latte Machiatto
accidentally - ausversehen
staring into space (exp) – ins Leere starren
berated - ausgezankt
scolded - ausgeschimpft

When Michael clocked out, he checked his phone and, sure enough, he had a text from the girl.

Hey! Meet me at Tony's Pizza at 7. See you there! ;)

Michael felt **giddy** as he responded to her text: *Okay! Looking forward to it. :)* And it was true, he really was looking forward to seeing the girl again. He had just enough time to go home, get cleaned up, and get a birthday card. Michael still lived with his parents at their house, which was close enough to **campus** that he could ride his bike. It was a beautiful day: sunny and not too hot. There was very little **traffic**, so his ride home was easy. He went inside the house, said hello to his mom, and went **upstairs** to change.

giddy - schwindlig
campus - Universitätsgelände
traffic - Verkehr
upstairs – Oben (Obergeschoss)

Michael was a very tall boy. He had just **turned** twenty-one, and his mom said he was probably finished growing. He was six and a half **feet** tall and sometimes it was hard to find trousers that were long enough. He had one nice pair of trousers that fit him perfectly, so he decided to wear them to meet the girl, even though he had also worn them to work and they smelled a little bit like **steamed** milk and coffee. He put on a red polo shirt, thinking that the girl might still be wearing her red blouse and it would be **funny** if they matched. To cover up the smell of coffee, Michael put on some **cologne** and then he was ready to leave.

turned – wurde (… Jahre alt)
feet - Fuß (hier, Maßeinheit)
steamed - gedämpft
funny - lustig
cologne - Parfüm

He had just enough time to stop by a **gift shop** on the way. He knew he had already given the girl the doughnut for a present, but he liked her a lot and wanted to **impress** her so he also got a card. He didn›t know what kind of card she would like, though! Would she want a card with a funny joke and a silly picture? Would she want a card with a **sentimental** message? Was she **religious**; would she want a card wishing her a **blessed** year? Michael settled on a card that was decorated with cute drawings of pink flowers and a happy **cartoon** puppy wishing her a happy birthday. He bought the card and started to write on it, but then he realized that he did not know her name!

gift shop - Geschenkladen
impress - beeindrucken
sentimental - gefühlvoll
religious - religiös
blessed - gesegnet
cartoon - Zeichentrick

Michael began to **panic**. How **stupid** could he be? He asked a girl **on a date** without even knowing her name! She had his phone number and everything. How **embarrassing**! Michael **groaned** out loud and thumped his head down on the counter.

"What's wrong, **buddy**?" The guy behind the counter was an older man with gray hair and glasses.

"I don't know this girl's name," Michael **moaned**. "I asked her on a date and I don't even know her name!"

"Tough luck, kiddo," the man said. He was trying not to laugh, but he thought it was **pretty funny**.

"I feel so **stupid**," Michael **grumbled**. "It's her birthday, too."

"Everyone makes **mistakes**," the man said, and he **shrugged**.

panic - Panik
stupid - dumm
on a date (exp) – nach einem Date
embarrassing - peinlich
groaned - stöhnte
buddy - Kumpel
moaned - jammern
pretty funny (exp) – ziemlich lustig
stupid - dumm

grumbled - motzen
mistakes - Fehler
shrugged - gezuckt

Michael decided he would just not write anything on the card and hope that she didn't **notice**. He had been feeling excited and happy all day, but now he just felt **nervous**. If she found out that he didn't know her name, she would probably think he was some kind of **creep** or maybe she would think he was stupid. Michael didn't know what she would think, but it probably would not be good!

He got on his bike with the blank birthday card in his backpack and started the ride to Tony's Pizza. *At least the food will be good,* he thought.

notice - gemerkt
nervous - nervös
creep – seltsamer Typ

Raquel was so happy about Michael coming to dinner that she almost **forgot** to eat her doughnut. She ate it during class and spilled a little bit of the **sweet cream filling** on her notebook. It wasn't **that big of a deal**, but her notebook would smell like pastries for weeks to come!

forgot - vergessen
sweet cream filling – süße Crèmefüllung
that big of a deal (exp) – war nicht so schlimm

The lecture was so boring that Raquel **barely** took any notes. It was a **statistics** class, and Raquel didn't really like math. She liked **history** class better, and this semester she was taking a **dance** class which she enjoyed a lot.

barely - kaum
statistics - Statistik
history - Geschichte
dance - tanzen

couldn't even enjoy her history lecture that day though, because she kept thinking about Michael. She kept thinking about his big, handsome, **goofy** smile. She thought about his black coffee shop **uniform** and wondered what he would wear later. She thought about his **shaggy** black hair. She thought about how tall he was, and she wondered if he had very big hands. She **wondered** if he would care that she was a whole **foot** shorter than him. She wondered about Michael all day long, until her last class ended and she was free to go.

goofy - albern
uniform - Uniform
shaggy - wuschelig
wondered - gewundert
foot - Fuß

She went to the library to do some **studying** but still kept thinking about Michael. She **texted** a bunch of her friends to invite them to dinner at Tony's Pizza later on, and after that she was able to study for a little bit, but Raquel really could not **focus** on her notes! So she decided to go take a walk because it was such a beautiful day.

studying - lernen
texted - schreiben
focus – fokussieren

Outside, the sky was a **deep blue** color and the air was cool and **refreshing**. It was **springtime**, so the grass and trees were a happy shade of green and there were flowers all over the place. Some of the trees had lots of tiny pink flowers, other trees had big white flowers, and some trees had no flowers at all: only **buds** and **leaves**. Bright yellow **daffodils** and **tulips** in a **multitude** of colors smiled up at Raquel from the ground, and because it was her birthday, she smiled right back.

deep blue – tiefes Blau
refreshing - erfrischend

springtime - Frühlingszeit
buds - Knospen
leaves - Blätter
daffodils - Narzissen
tulips - Tulpen
multitude - mehrere

Raquel saw a few of her friends while she was walking, and asked them to come to her birthday dinner later that night, but they all said they were busy! Jolisa had to work, Mary Beth had an **exam** the next day, Carrie had a **paperdue**, and Thomas had to take his cat to the **veterinarian**. Raquel felt **disappointed** but it was still her birthday, so she tried not to let it **get her down**.

exam - Prüfung
paper due – Abgabedatum
veterinarian - Tierarzt
disappointed - enttäuscht
get her down – sie runterziehen

At last, seven o'clock **came around**. Raquel walked in to Tony's Pizza and chose a great big table so that everyone she had invited could sit with her. She ordered a soda and **eagerly** watched the door, waiting for her friends **to show up**.

But they didn't.

Seven o'clock became seven-thirty, and then it was eight o'clock. Raquel drank three sodas and was still sitting all by herself at the great, big, empty table. She tried not to be sad but, when eight o'clock came and no one was there to celebrate with her, Raquel felt **tears** in her eyes and she looked down at the table.

"Hey!" said a **familiar** voice.

Raquel looked up and saw Michael standing beside her. He looked very nice in his red polo shirt, except he had a **scrape** on his arm and his hair was **mussed**!

"What happened?" Raquel **cried**, **leaping** to her feet. "Are you okay?"

came around – kam an
eagerly -eifrig
to show up - aufkreuzen
tears - Tränen
familiar - bekannt
scrape -Kratzer
mussed - zerzaust
cried - weinte
leaping - sprang auf

"Yeah, I just **crashed** my bicycle," Michael said **sheepishly**, "that's why I'm late. I'm really sorry."

"**Oh my gosh**. You're not hurt, are you?"

"No, I'm fine! I promise. Um... where is everyone else?" Michael asked. He looked at the empty table with a **concerned expression**.

crashed – zerschmettert
sheepishly - verlegen
Oh my gosh – oh mein Gott
concerned - besorgtem
expression - Ausdruck

"That is a good question," Raquel grumbled. "No one showed up."

"Let me buy you some pizza," Michael offered as he and Raquel sat down together.

Together, Michael and Raquel finished a whole pepperoni pizza. It was the best pizza either of them had ever tasted. Raquel felt much better after she ate, and she thanked Michael for coming to dinner.

"**It's my pleasure**," Michael told her, "I've been **looking forward to it** all day!" He took the card out of his backpack and handed it to her, "For you."

"Thank you!" Raquel exclaimed. She opened the card, and as she read it, she smiled. "That's **so sweet of you**, Michael."

Michael smiled and **squirmed** a little in his seat when she said his name, because he still didn't know her name. He had asked her on a date, bought her dinner, and given her a birthday card; and he still didn't know her name! The evening ended after they sat and talked for a few hours. They both had class early the next day and needed to get home and go to bed.

"Let me give you a ride home, since your bike is broken," Raquel **offered**. Michael **agreed**, and she drove him home. Once they got to Michael's house, Raquel said, "Thanks again, Michael, this was the best birthday I've ever had!"

Michael smiled and, feeling **brave**, he leaned over and **kissed** the girl's **cheek**!

Raquel giggled. Michael said goodnight and went inside. *He still didn't know her name.*

"How was your date, **honey**?" Michael's mom asked when he came in.

"It was... good," Michael said.

"You don't seem too sure about that," his mother said, looking at him over the top of her glasses.

"Mom?"

"Yes?"

"I don't know her name. The girl I asked out. I don't know her name! I forgot to get it when I met her, but she knows my name and she has my number and everything," Michael **groaned**.

"Why don't you just ask her?" his mom said.

"I can't just ask her! She'll think I'm so dumb!" Michael said.

"If she is the right girl for you, she'll understand," Michael's mom **reassured** him, but this didn't make Michael feel any better. "Can you ask one of her friends?"

"I can't just ask someone!" Michael **scoffed**, "They might tell her."

"Didn't you say you have a class with her? Maybe you can ask the professor," his mom **suggested**.

So, the next day during his class with the girl Michael **approached** the professor and asked for the girl's name. He **described** Raquel, but Michael wasn't very good at describing, and the professor thought he meant a different girl!

"Her name is Brittany," the professor said **confidently**.

When the girl walked in the room, Michael **marched** right up to her and smiled.

"Hi, Brittany," he said. His smile went away as the girl **frowned**.

"My name is Raquel," she grumbled.

Michael was **mortified**. He felt about **as tall as a grasshopper's knee**. He wanted to disappear into the floor. His cheeks turned bright red. Raquel saw how embarrassed he was and she **relaxed**.

"That's okay, Michael. Everyone makes mistakes!" Raquel took his hand and they sat down together in the front row.

Best Birthday Ever

Raquel thought that Michael was the best birthday present she had ever gotten.

It's my pleasure (exp) – Es ist mir ein Vergnügen
looking forward to it (exp) - die ganze Zeit darauf freuen
so sweet of you (exp) – so süß von dir
squirmed - wand sich
offered - bot an
agreed - stimmte zu
brave - mutig
kissed - küsste
cheek - Wange
honey - Honig
groaned - stöhnte
reassured -sichergehen
scoffed -verspottet
suggested - vorschlagen
approached - zugehen
described - beschreiben
confidently - selbstsicher
marched - marschieren
frowned - runzelte die Stirn
mortified - beschämt
as tall as a grasshopper›s knee (exp) – sich sehr klein fühlen
relaxed - entspannt

Vocabulary:

like a million bucks (exp) – wie ne´ Millionen Dollar zu haben (Redewendung)
Went off – ging aus
morning person (exp) – Morgenmüffel
amazing - erstaunlich
stretched - streckte
yawn - gähnen
good hair day (exp) – Gute-Frisur-Tag
mind of its own (exp) – eigenwillig war
baby blue – Babyblau
bouncy ponytail – lockerer Pferdeschwanz
fancy - schick
makeup - Schminke
applied - auftragen
eyeliner - Eyeliner
fashion magazines – Mode-Zeitschriften
mascara - Wimperntusche
eyelashes - Wimpern
lipstick - Lippenstift
fashionable - modisch
festive - festlich
blouse - Bluse
ballerina skirt – Ballerina Rock
flats – Ballerinas (Schuhart, meist getragen beim Ballett)
kitchenette - Kochniesche
brewing - kochte
indulge -verwöhnen
pastry - Gebäck
Boston cream doughnut – Boston Crème Donut
handsome – gutaussehend (Mann)
Boy (exp) - Mensch
promotion - Aktion
erupted - ausbrechen
giggles - kichern
blushed – erröten
exclaimed - ausgerufen

shyly - schüchtern
beamed - strahlte
awesome - wundervoll
ridiculously - lächerlich
text - schreibe
See you later (exp) – Bis Später
admiring - bewundern
dizzy - schwindelig
hardly believe (exp) – nicht glauben können
stranger - Fremder
shift - Schicht
butterflies in his stomach (exp) – Schmetterlinge im Bauch
flirted - geflirtet
Time slowed to a crawl (exp) – die Zeit blieb fast stehen
burned - verbrannt
latte – Latte Machiatto
accidentally - ausversehen
staring into space (exp) – ins Leere starren
berated - ausgezankt
scolded - ausgeschimpft
giddy - schwindlig
campus - Universitätsgelände
traffic - Verkehr
upstairs – Oben (Obergeschoss)
turned – wurde (… Jahre alt)
feet - Fuß (hier, Maßeinheit)
steamed - gedämpft
funny - lustig
cologne - Parfüm
gift shop - Geschenkladen
impress - beeindrucken
sentimental - gefühlvoll
religious - religiös
blessed - gesegnet
cartoon - Zeichentrick
panic - Panik
stupid - dumm
on a date (exp) – nach einem Date

embarrassing - peinlich
groaned - stöhnte
buddy - Kumpel
moaned - jammern
pretty funny (exp) – ziemlich lustig
stupid - dumm
grumbled - motzen
mistakes - Fehler
shrugged - gezuckt
notice - gemerkt
nervous - nervös
creep – seltsamer Typ
forgot - vergessen
sweet cream filling – süße Crèmefüllung
that big of a deal (exp) – war nicht so schlimm
barely - kaum
statistics - Statistik
history - Geschichte
dance - tanzen
goofy - albern
uniform - Uniform
shaggy - wuschelig
wondered - gewundert
foot - Fuß
studying - lernen
texted - schreiben
focus – fokussieren
deep blue – tiefes Blau
refreshing - erfrischend
springtime - Frühlingszeit
buds - Knospen
leaves - Blätter
daffodils - Narzissen
tulips - Tulpen
multitude - mehrere
exam - Prüfung
paper due – Abgabedatum
veterinarian - Tierarzt

disappointed - enttäuscht
get her down – sie runterziehen
came around – kam an
eagerly -eifrig
to show up - aufkreuzen
tears - Tränen
familiar - bekannt
scrape -Kratzer
mussed - zerzaust
cried - weinte
leaping - sprang auf
crashed – zerschmettert
sheepishly - verlegen
Oh my gosh – oh mein Gott
concerned - besorgtem
expression - Ausdruck
It›s my pleasure (exp) – Es ist mir ein Vergnügen
looking forward to it (exp) - die ganze Zeit darauf freuen
so sweet of you (exp) – so süß von dir
squirmed - wand sich
offered - bot an
agreed - stimmte zu
brave - mutig
kissed - küsste
cheek - Wange
honey - Honig
groaned - stöhnte
reassured -sichergehen
scoffed -verspottet
suggested - vorschlagen
approached - zugehen
described - beschreiben
confidently - selbstsicher
marched - marschieren
frowned - runzelte die Stirn
mortified - beschämt
as tall as a grasshopper›s knee (exp) – sich sehr klein fühlen
relaxed - entspannt

Holidays in America

American **holidays** are **strange** to me. I was **born and raised** on the East Coast in America. I have lived through these holidays all of my life, and with each year I only see them as stranger and stranger. Some of our holidays have special **religious** meaning, but some of them do not. All of them are **associated** with interesting **traditions**.

holidays - Feiertage
strange - komisch
born and raised (exp) - aufgewachsen
religious - religiös
associated - dazugehörig
traditions - Traditionen

It all starts on the first of January: **New Year's Day**. It is a **public holiday**, which means that most businesses and offices will be closed for the whole day. Some people call the 1st of January, "National **Hangover** Day," because it is traditional to **drink too much** on the 31st of December: New Year's Eve. I wonder why someone would want to start the New Year feeling **sick**. New Year's Day is **special** to me because I really like the idea of an **official** date to **start over** or begin **working** to **achieve** a **goal**. I like new **beginnings**. New Year's Day did not mean much to me when I was **growing up**, but now that I'm older, I understand better the **healing** power of a **formal** new beginning. When we **make mistakes** as children, maybe we get yelled at by our parents, or we get a **time-out**, but then the mistake is over and done with. We move on quickly. As adults, when we make mistakes they tend to be big mistakes that follow us around for a long time. New Year's Day, gives us a chance to **wipe the slate clean**. Even if we are still **dealing with** the **consequences** of our mistakes, we can try to **forgive** ourselves and leave the **regret** behind in the old year.

New Year's Day - Neujahrstag
public holiday (exp) - gesetzlicher Feiertag
Hangover – Kater
drink too much (exp) – zu viel getrunken
sick - übel
special - besonders
official - offiziell
start over(exp) - Neuanfang
working - arbeiten
achieve - erreichen
goal - Ziel
beginnings - Anfänge
growing up - aufwachsen
healing - heilend
formal - formell
make mistakes (exp) – Fehler machen
time-out - Auszeit
wipe (exp) - wischen
the slate clean (exp) - reinen Tisch machen
dealing with (exp) – umgehen mit
consequences - Konsequenzen
forgive - vergeben
regret - bereuen

Martin Luther King Jr. Day is **celebrated** on the third Monday in January. It is also a public holiday, so many offices are closed. This day honors a black **activist** from the 1960s who helped peacefully advance the causes of **civil rights** and **racial equality** in the United States. Despite the cultural significance of the person the day celebrates, this holiday is not as popular as many of the others in this country.

celebrated - gefeiert
activist - Aktivist
peacefully advance – friedliches Voranschreiten
civil rights – Zivilrechte
racial equality - Rassengleichheit
cultural significance – kultureller Sinn

Valentine's Day is celebrated on the 14th of February. It is not a public holiday, which means that offices and businesses do not close, but Valentine's Day is a pretty big part of American culture. It is a special day **set aside** for **romantic couples** to celebrate one another and offer **displays** of love and **affection**. Traditional Valentine's Day gifts are flowers, **cards**, **candy** (especially **chocolate**), and sometimes **jewelry** or **stuffed animals**. Many couples arrange a special **date** on Valentine's Day and have dinner at a **fancy** restaurant. When I was a kid, we used to exchange Valentine's cards at school, but we were not **allowed** to just bring a Valentine's card for someone we **had a crush on**. We had to bring cards for everyone in the class so that no one **felt left out**. Some people would also bring in candy which was very exciting! Now that I'm older, I think Valentine's Day is a bit **silly** because I think we should show our love and affection to the people we care about every day of the year. Other people don't like Valentine's Day because it makes people who are **single** feel left out. Even when I am single on Valentine's Day (which I am right now!), I like the holiday because I like to feel **festive**. Last year, I took myself out to a fancy dinner on Valentine's Day. It was probably the best Valentine's Day I've ever had.

Valentine's Day - Valentinstag
set aside (exp) - zur Seite gelegt
romantic couples – romantische Paare
displays - zeigen
affection - Zuneigung
cards - Karten
candy - Süssigkeiten
chocolate - Schokolade
jewelry - Schmuck
stuffed animals - Stofftiere
date - ausgehen
fancy - modern
allowed - erlaubt
had a crush on (exp) – verliebt sein
felt left out (exp) - ausgeschlossen fühlt
silly - albern

single - Single, ledig
festive - festlich

President's Day is celebrated on the third Monday in February. Even though it is a public holiday and we **get the day off**, it is not as culturally significant as some of the other holidays. This day **commemorates** the first **president** of the United States, George Washington, and other **influential** presidents from our history.

President's Day – Tag des Präsidenten
get the day off (exp) - den Tag frei bekommen
commemorates - gedenkt
president - Präsident
influential - einflussreich

On the 17ty of March we celebrate **Saint Patrick›s Day**. Originally, Saint Patrick›s Day was one of the **Catholic feast** days which **recognize** various **saints** within the Catholic **religion** and commemorate their **contributions**. However, in the **present day** Saint Patrick›s Day is also celebrated by people who are not Catholic as a day for people to wear the color green, eat and drink green-colored food, and celebrate Irish **heritage** (Saint Patrick is the **patron saint** of Ireland). Many people also drink alcohol on Saint Patrick›s Day. There is a tradition that if a person is not wearing green on Saint Patrick›s Day, you are supposed to **pinch** them. There are also **legends** about tiny **mythical creatures** called **leprechauns**, which resemble **fairies**, and if you catch a leprechaun it has to give you a pot of **gold**. When I was very young, we set up a "leprechaun trap" at school! The next morning, we came in and there was no gold, but there was a set of tiny green **footprints** leading away from the trap - the "leprechaun" had **escaped**!

Saint Patrick›s Day - Saint Patrick´s Day
Catholic feast - Katholisches Festmahl
recognize - anerkennen
saints - Heiligen

religion - Religion
contributions - Spenden
present day - Gegenwart
heritage - Erbe
patron saint (exp) - Schutzheilige
pinch - kneifen
legends - Legenden
mythical creatures - mythische Kreaturen
leprechauns - Kobolde
fairies - Feen
gold - Gold
footprints - Fußabdrücke
escaped - geflohen

In late March or early April we celebrate **Easter Sunday** which is another holiday **rooted** in religious tradition. In **popular culture**, Saint Patrick›s Day has lost much of its religious **meaning**, but Easter is still mostly a religious holiday. Many Christian people go to **church** on Easter Sunday regardless of what **denomination** they are. Some non-Christian people celebrate Easter Sunday simply because holidays are fun! Easter is a traditional time to have a big dinner with the family or sometimes with **extended family**. A classic Easter dinner might be **ham**, served with **vegetables** and **breadon the side**. Small children are given toys and candy as symbols of the **bounty** and **fertility** of **springtime**. Other symbols of spring, like **rabbits**, are also associated with Easter Sunday. Chocolate in the shape of rabbits and **marshmallows** shaped like baby birds are also **consumed**. There is a myth that on Easter Sunday, the Easter bunny brings the gifts of toys and candy to the children. Though today, Easter is a **predominantly** Christian holiday, it also has interesting **elements** of old **Pagan** celebrations of **nature** and springtime. It is one of two very important holidays in the United States like that.

Easter Sunday – Ostersonntag
rooted - verwurzelt
popular culture (exp) - beliebte Kultur
meaning - Bedeutung

church - Kirche
denomination - Konfession
extended family – umfassende Familie
ham - Schinken
vegetables - Gemüse
bread on the side – Brotbeilage
bounty - Beute
fertility - Fruchtbarkeit
springtime - Frühlingszeit
rabbits - Hasen
consumed - konsumieren
marshmallows - Mäusespeck
predominantly - überwiegend
elements - Elemente
Pagan - heidnisch
nature - Natur

At the end of May, there is a public holiday called **Memorial Day**. This holiday is meant to commemorate all of the people who have **served** in the **military** and honor those who lost their lives in service. It is interesting to me that, in this country, we pay less attention to more **serious** holidays like this one. Memorial Day is not as culturally significant as some of the other holidays like, for example, Valentine›s Day.

Memorial Day – Volkstrauertag (Heldengedenktag)
served - gedient
military - Militär
serious - ernsthaft

At the **beginning** of July, we celebrate **Independence Day**. Independence Day is a public holiday on the fourth of July which commemorates the **signing** of the **document** that **declared** the United States› **independence** from Great Britain. Traditionally, we **set off fireworks** at night to celebrate, and some communities have big, **impressive** displays of fireworks for everyone to watch. When I was growing up, a family friend used to have a **huge party** every year for Independence

Day, and I remember that it was always lots of fun. **Dozens** of people came and went all day long. Everyone brought food to share, and they made **barbecue** on a **charcoal grill**. Barbecues are a popular way to celebrate Independence Day. My favorite part of those parties was always the **squirt gunfights**! They would set up a small **plastic kiddie pool** full of water, leave a **bunch** of toy squirt guns there, and my friends and I would have **epic battles** in the hot July sun until we were all **soaking** wet. Sometimes the battles would last until **twilight**, and then we would be called away to watch the fireworks. We could see big fireworks from the back yard, so everyone would gather in the back to watch the big **community display** from far away. Then we would all move to the front yard, where they would set off a bunch of smaller fireworks in the **driveway**. I haven›t been to that party in years, but I would bet it still happens!

beginning - Anfang
Independence Day - Unabhängigkeitstag
signing - unterschreiben
document - Dokument
declared - erklärt
independence - Unabhängigkeit
set off (exp) - anzünden
fireworks - Feuerwerk
impressive - beeindruckend
huge party – große Feier
Dozens - dutzende
barbecue - Grillen
charcoal grill – Kohlegrill
squirt gun fights – Wasserpistolenschlacht
plastic kiddie pool - Planschbecken
bunch - viele
epic battles – krasse kämpfe
soaking - eingeweicht
twilight - Dämmerung
community display – Gemeinde Präsentation
driveway - Einfahrt

In September, we have another public holiday called **Labor Day** which is **supposed** to commemorate the contributions of the **Labor** Movement which helped **establish workers› rights** in the United States. This was a very important movement, but I **doubt** many Americans know what Labor Day is supposed to celebrate!

Labor Day – Tag der Arbeit
supposed - sollte
Labor - Arbeit
establish workers› rights – Arbeiterrechte gründen
doubt - zweifle

At the end of October, we celebrate **Halloween** on the last day of the month. Halloween is a **blend** of **various** religious traditions that has become, like most other major holidays in the United States, simplified by its **popularity**. It is not a public holiday. Halloween is meant to celebrate the **memory** of people who have **passed on**, but I think it has lost that meaning for most people. **Nowadays**, Halloween is a day to dress in **costumes**, **throw parties**, give out candy, and even **pull pranks**! Many children dress in costumes and go to each house in their **neighborhood** to collect candy in a tradition known as “trick-or-treating.” When the neighbor opens the door, the children are supposed to say, “Trick or treat!” Originally, this meant that if the person did not wish to be “**tricked**”, they had to give the children a “**treat**” such as candy. I think that most people do not even **bother** with playing tricks anymore. It is now **expected** that people **give out** the candy. As a grown person, I think it›s a lot of fun to **hand out** candy to children and see all of their costumes. Halloween was my favorite holiday as a child because I loved **dressing up** - this is still true for me today, even though I do not get candy any more. Most children stop “trick-or-treating” as adolescents. Another fun Halloween tradition is **pumpkin carving**. People buy pumpkin **gourds** and **hollow** them out by **scooping** out the **seeds** and **pulp**. A **design** is carved in to the hollow pumpkin so that a **candle** can be **inserted** and the design will light up at night. The carved designs are sometimes **spooky** but sometimes also very beautiful.

Halloween - Halloween
blend - Mischung
various - unterschiedlichen
popularity - Beliebtheit
memory - Erinnerung
passed on (exp) - verstorben sind
Nowadays – Heutzutage
costumes - Kostüme
throw parties (exp) - Partys veranstalten
pull pranks (exp) - Streiche spielen
neighborhood - Nachbarschaft
tricked - ausgetrickst
treat - Belohnung
bother - beschäftigen
expected - erwartet
give out (exp) - ausgeben
hand out (exp) - verteilen
dressing up (exp) - verkleiden
pumpkin carving – Kürbis Schnitzen
gourds - Kürbisgewächs
hollow - hohl
scooping - auslöffeln
seeds - Samen
pulp - Fruchtfleisch
design - Design
candle - Kerze
inserted - einsetzen
spooky - gruselig

The third Thursday in November marks a holiday called **Thanksgiving**. This holiday has its origins in the country›s history as well, and it is supposed to celebrate the first **harvest** when the **colonists** came to the **continent**. The **cornucopia** is a **symbol** of Thanksgiving **representing** the thanks being given for the **abundance** that we enjoy. The turkey is also a symbol of the **Thanksgiving** holiday because it is the traditional **centerpiece** of the Thanksgiving meal. The turkey is typically **stuffed** with **seasoned bread crumbs** before **baking** and the **stuffing** is served as a side dish along with **cranberry** sauce and some vegetables, like string beans or collard greens. This is another holiday where it is traditional for the whole family to **get together** for a big meal. It is a public holiday, and some say it is the most-traveled day of the year, as people drive to see their relatives. The day after Thanksgiving is a popular time for stores to **have sales** encouraging people to start buying gifts for Christmas which is usually about one month afterward. I have always thought it was a bit silly to start **anticipating** Christmas so early, but many people put up Christmas lights and buy Christmas trees the day after Thanksgiving.

Thanksgiving - Erntedankfest
harvest - Ernte
colonists - Kolonisten
continent - Kontinent
cornucopia - Füllhorn
symbol - Symbol
representing - vertretend
abundance -Reichtum
centerpiece – Herzstück
stuffed - gestopft
seasoned breadcrumbs – gewürzte Brotkrümmel
baking - backen
stuffing - Füllung
cranberry – Preiselbeere
get together (exp) - sich treffen
have sales (exp) - haben Anbegote
anticipating - erwarten

As you might have guessed, **Christmas** is a **very big deal** in the United States. It is a public holiday celebrated on the 25th of December, and it is probably the very biggest holiday of them all for most people. Some stores start **displaying** Christmas **merchandise** the day after Halloween, almost two months **in advance**! Christmas is like Easter, in that it is a blend of Christian and Pagan traditions, but presently it is recognized mostly as a Christian holiday. Many people go to church at Christmas. I mentioned **Christmas trees** earlier, which are a Pagan tradition of bringing **evergreen branches indoors** to make the home more **cheerful** in the winter. In the **modern** version of this tradition: people buy whole evergreen trees, set them up in their homes, and decorate them with lights and **ornaments**. Festive Christmas lights are also put up on the **exterior** of the house. Some neighborhoods even have Christmas light **competitions** to see who can make the biggest, best display! **Gift-giving** is another big part of the Christmas holiday, but some people feel that this **detracts** from the religious meaning of the holiday. Part of the gift-giving tradition is the **myth** of Santa Claus who was a religious figure in Europe. Through years of re-telling and **commercializing** the European religious story, we wound up with a myth about a man in a red suit who comes into the house on Christmas Eve to leave gifts for children while they sleep. **For some reason**, many children are **raised** to believe that this myth is true, and that Santa Claus is a real person. This might be because Santa Claus is not supposed to leave gifts for children who are **naughty**! Christmas was always very important in my family, because it is a major holiday, but it is also my father›s **birthday** and my grandmother›s birthday! Many families get together for a big Christmas dinner which typically includes turkey or ham with the usual bread and vegetables on the side. In my family, we also get to have **birthday cake**!

Christmas - Weihnachten
very big deal (exp) - sehr große Sache
displaying - vorstellen
merchandise - Ware
in advance (exp) - viel früher
Christmas trees - Weihnachtsbäume
evergreen branches indoors – Nadelbaumzweige innen
cheerful - fröhlich
modern -modern
ornaments - Ornamente
exterior - äußere
competitions - Wettbewerbe
Gift-giving – Geschenke geben

detracts - abziehen
myth - Sage
commercializing - kommerzialisieren
For some reason (exp) - aus irgendeinem Grund
raised - aufgewachsen
naughty - ungezogen
birthday - Geburtstag
birthday cake – Geburtstagskuchen

A few days after Christmas, on the 31st of December, we celebrate **New Year›s Eve**. Many people stay up until **midnight** to **welcome** the New Year. There is a large, **famous** celebration that happens in New York City on New Year›s Eve every year. Thousands of people **congregate** in Times Square to "watch the ball drop." The ball sits **atop** a **pole** on top of a **building** in Times Square, and is slowly **lowered** over sixty seconds so that it lands at **exactly** midnight. Almost everyone **counts down** the last ten seconds of the year, and then, at midnight people blow **noisemakers** and sing a song called "Auld Lang Syne." This is a Scottish song known widely in the English-speaking world for welcoming the New Year. There are many traditions across many cultures **surrounding** the New Year, but a very popular one (other than the "ball drop") is that you›re supposed to **kiss** someone at midnight! I›m not sure why this is, but I have never done it and my years have all turned out pretty good anyway. Some people also do a **champagne** toast at midnight.

New Year›s Eve - Silvester
midnight - Mitternacht
welcome - Willkommen heißen
famous - berühmt
congregate - zusammenkommen
atop – oben drauf
pole - Stange
building - Gebäude
lowered - gesenkt
exactly - genau
counts down (exp) - zählen runter

noisemakers - Krachmacher
surrounding - umgeben
kiss - Kuss
champagne - Champagner

That **completes** the **cycle** of **weird** holidays and fun traditions! The next day is New Year›s Day: a new beginning, a fresh start, and a clean slate.

completes - vervollständigt
cycle - Kreis
weird - seltsam

Vocabulary

holidays - Feiertage
strange - komisch
born and raised (exp) - aufgewachsen
religious - religiös
associated - dazugehörig
traditions - Traditionen
New Year›s Day - Neujahrstag
public holiday (exp) - gesetzlicher Feiertag
Hangover – Kater
drink too much (exp) – zu viel getrunken
sick - übel
special - besonders
official - offiziell
start over(exp) - Neuanfang
working - arbeiten
achieve - erreichen
goal - Ziel
beginnings - Anfänge
growing up - aufwachsen
healing - heilend
formal - formell
make mistakes (exp) – Fehler machen
time-out - Auszeit
wipe (exp) - wischen
the slate clean (exp) - reinen Tisch machen
dealing with (exp) – umgehen mit
consequences - Konsequenzen
forgive - vergeben
regret - bereuen
celebrated - gefeiert
activist - Aktivist
peacefully advance – friedliches Voranschreiten
civil rights – Zivilrechte
racial equality - Rassengleichheit
cultural significance – kultureller Sinn

Valentine›s Day - Valentinstag
set aside (exp) - zur Seite gelegt
romantic couples – romantische Paare
displays - zeigen
affection - Zuneigung
cards - Karten
candy - Süssigkeiten
chocolate - Schokolade
jewelry - Schmuck
stuffed animals - Stofftiere
date - ausgehen
fancy - modern
allowed - erlaubt
had a crush on (exp) – verliebt sein
felt left out (exp) - ausgeschlossen fühlt
silly - albern
single - Single, ledig
festive - festlich
President›s Day – Tag des Präsidenten
get the day off (exp) - den Tag frei bekommen
commemorates - gedenkt
president - Präsident
influential - einflussreich
Saint Patrick›s Day - Saint Patrick´s Day
Catholic feast - Katholisches Festmahl
recognize - anerkennen
saints - Heiligen
religion - Religion
contributions - Spenden
present day - Gegenwart
heritage - Erbe
patron saint (exp) - Schutzheilige
pinch - kneifen
legends - Legenden
mythical creatures - mythische Kreaturen
leprechauns - Kobolde
fairies - Feen
gold - Gold

footprints - Fußabdrücke
escaped - geflohen
Easter Sunday – Ostersonntag
rooted - verwurzelt
popular culture (exp) - beliebte Kultur
meaning - Bedeutung
church - Kirche
denomination - Konfession
extended family – umfassende Familie
ham - Schinken
vegetables - Gemüse
bread on the side – Brotbeilage
bounty - Beute
fertility - Fruchtbarkeit
springtime - Frühlingszeit
rabbits - Hasen
consumed - konsumieren
marshmallows - Mäusespeck
predominantly - überwiegend
elements - Elemente
Pagan - heidnisch
nature - Natur
Memorial Day – Volkstrauertag (Heldengedenktag)
served - gedient
military - Militär
serious - ernsthaft
beginning - Anfang
Independence Day - Unabhängigkeitstag
signing - unterschreiben
document - Dokument
declared - erklärt
independence - Unabhängigkeit
set off (exp) - anzünden
fireworks - Feuerwerk
impressive - beeindruckend
huge party – große Feier
Dozens - dutzende
barbecue - Grillen

charcoal grill – Kohlegrill
squirt gun fights – Wasserpistolenschlacht
plastic kiddie pool - Planschbecken
bunch - viele
epic battles – krasse kämpfe
soaking - eingeweicht
twilight - Dämmerung
community display – Gemeinde Präsentation
driveway - Einfahrt
Labor Day – Tag der Arbeit
supposed - sollte
Labor - Arbeit
establish workers› rights – Arbeiterrechte gründen
doubt - zweifle
Halloween - Halloween
blend - Mischung
various - unterschiedlichen
popularity - Beliebtheit
memory - Erinnerung
passed on (exp) - verstorben sind
Nowadays – Heutzutage
costumes - Kostüme
throw parties (exp) - Partys veranstalten
pull pranks (exp) - Streiche spielen
neighborhood - Nachbarschaft
tricked - ausgetrickst
treat - Belohnung
bother - beschäftigen
expected - erwartet
give out (exp) - ausgeben
hand out (exp) - verteilen
dressing up (exp) - verkleiden
pumpkin carving – Kürbis Schnitzen
gourds - Kürbisgewächs
hollow - hohl
scooping - auslöffeln
seeds - Samen
pulp - Fruchtfleisch

design - Design
candle - Kerze
inserted - einsetzen
spooky - gruselig
Thanksgiving - Erntedankfest
harvest - Ernte
colonists - Kolonisten
continent - Kontinent
cornucopia - Füllhorn
symbol - Symbol
representing - vertretend
abundance -Reichtum
centerpiece – Herzstück
stuffed - gestopft
seasoned breadcrumbs – gewürzte Brotkrümmel
baking - backen
stuffing - Füllung
cranberry – Preiselbeere
get together (exp) - sich treffen
have sales (exp) - haben Anbegote
anticipating - erwarten
Christmas - Weihnachten
very big deal (exp) - sehr große Sache
displaying - vorstellen
merchandise - Ware
in advance (exp) - viel früher
Christmas trees - Weihnachtsbäume
evergreen branches indoors – Nadelbaumzweige innen
cheerful - fröhlich
modern -modern
ornaments - Ornamente
exterior - äußere
competitions - Wettbewerbe
Gift-giving – Geschenke geben
detracts - abziehen
myth - Sage
commercializing - kommerzialisieren
For some reason (exp) - aus irgendeinem Grund

raised - aufgewachsen
naughty - ungezogen
birthday - Geburtstag
birthday cake – Geburtstagskuchen
New Year›s Eve - Silvester
midnight - Mitternacht
welcome - Willkommen heißen
famous - berühmt
congregate - zusammenkommen
atop – oben drauf
pole - Stange
building - Gebäude
lowered - gesenkt
exactly - genau
counts down (exp) - zählen runter
noisemakers - Krachmacher
surrounding - umgeben
kiss - Kuss
champagne - Champagner
completes - vervollständigt
cycle - Kreis
weird - seltsam

Love Yourself

"I have to find the perfect dress for **prom** next week!" Laila **sighed** as she passed racks of beautiful dresses. This one was **champagne-colored**, with a **gauzy** skirt that went all the way to the floor. The other one was bright pink, and the skirt was short and sort of **poofy**. That one was **turquoise-colored**, and it had lots of shiny **crystals** sewn into a pattern on the **bust**. Laila **admired** them all, but she knew she could not have them because they didn't sell them in her size.

prom - Ball
sighed - seufzte
champagne-colored – champagnerfarbig
gauzy - hauchdünn
poofy - tuntenhaft
turquoise-colored – türkisfarbend
crystals – Glitzersteine
bust - Brust
admired - bewundert

Laila was fat.

She followed her mom to the **plus sized** part of the store. The clothes that fit Laila were designed for much older people. She was only sixteen, and she wanted to wear a **sparkly**, shiny dress like all the other girls would be wearing, and she felt so sad that she could not.

"What about this one, **honey**?" Laila's mom held up... a suit. A **business** suit. A pale pink **blazer** and a knee-length skirt. Laila **groaned** out loud.

"I'll look like an old woman!" she **protested**. She turned to **peruse** the selection of other dresses. They all looked like clothes that a grandma would wear to **church** on Sunday. She settled on an **olive green** dress with deep pink roses **embroidered** on the **neckline**, **sleeves**, and skirt.

"You'll look so nice in that," Laila's mom said.

"**It's okay**, I **guess**," Laila **grumbled**. She knew she would be **embarrassed** no matter what she wore, because she was fat, and everyone could see it.

plus size (exp) – XXL-Abteilung
sparkly - schimmernd
honey - Honig
business - Geschäft
blazer - Blazer
groaned - stöhnte
protested - protestierte
peruse - durchgehen
church - Kirche
olive green – olivgrün
embroidered - bestickt
neckline - Ausschnitt
sleeves - Ärmel
It's okay (exp) – es ist okay
I guess (exp) – ich denke
grumbled - grummeln
embarrassed - peinlich

All her life, it had been difficult for Laila to find clothes. It was the same, every time, whether she needed a prom dress or a new pair of jeans. She had to **compromise** between what she liked and what would fit her. It was always a long, painful **chore** that left Laila feeling **exhausted** and **depressed**.

compromise - Kompromisse eingehen
chore - Aufgabe
exhausted - ermüdet
depressed - deprimiert

Many stores did not carry clothes in her size. Laila felt like the world was saying that fat people did not **deserve** nice, **stylish** clothes, and that was why there were none in the stores. Some stores **exclusively** had clothes made for fat people, but those clothes were often very **expensive**, poorly made, and in a style that looked more like a dull **middle-aged divorcee** than a teen aged girl. Kids at school **made fun of her** because she was fat, and they made fun of her because of the clothes she was **forced** to wear because they did not make clothes for girls Laila's size and age. Every day, she looked in the mirror and felt sad looking at herself. It was not easy to be fat.

deserve - verdient
stylish – schick, modern
exclusively - exklusive
expensive - teuer
middle-aged divorcee – geschieden im mittleren Alter
made (exp) - gemacht
fun of her (exp) - ausgelacht
forced - gezwungen

People who cared about Laila said things to her that hurt her feelings. They all **meant well**, but really, they just made Laila feel worse and worse about herself!

"You don't need to eat that," Laila's mother would say, even if Laila was really hungry.

"But I'm hungry," Laila would **counter**.

"Hunger hurts, but **starving** works," her mother sometimes said, so Laila would go hungry. Sometimes she would go so long without eating that she would feel **dizzy**, and sometimes she would **faint**, but no one believed that it was because she had not eaten. Then kids made fun of Laila for being fat and for fainting.

meant well (exp) – gut gemeint
counter - entgegnen

starving - verhungern
dizzy - schwindelig
faint – Ohnmächtig werden

"Boys would like you if you lost weight," Laila's dad said, which made Laila feel like no one would ever like her unless she lost weight. There was a boy at school that Laila **had a crush on**, but she rarely spoke to him because she was so sure he would not even look at a girl like her. **Little did Laila know**, the boy **liked her** too, but because Laila never spoke to him, he thought that Laila hated him!

had a crush on (exp) – verliebt sein
Little did Laila know (exp) – aber Laila wusste nicht
liked her (exp) – mochte sie

"You'd have more friends if you were thinner," Laila's grandma said, even though Laila did have friends who liked her just the way she was. Did her grandma mean that her friends secretly did not like Laila because she was fat?

Ever since she was very young, Laila did not like herself. As young as six years old, Laila would see herself in the mirror and feel bad. Was it because of her size, Laila wondered, or because of how people treated her because of her size? It had to be because of her size because everyone else blamed her size, Laila reasoned. Fat was bad, she was fat, and that made her bad.

As she got a little older, Laila started **going on diets**. She went on her first diet at age ten, and all she was allowed to eat was **spinach**: **Raw** spinach, **cooked** spinach, **steamed** spinach, **roasted** spinach... Laila could eat as much spinach as she wanted, but nothing else. The diet gave her a stomach ache and she could only **stick with it** for one week. After that, the sight of spinach made Laila feel a little **queasy** in her stomach. She tried other diets too, one right after the other, and they all had **strange** names and very **specific** rules. One diet only allowed **cabbage** soup and **grapefruit** for two meals a day, but the third meal could be whatever she wanted. One diet only allowed meat, eggs, and dairy, but fruit, grains, and most vegetables were **forbidden**! It was strange to Laila that she could have as much cheese as she wanted but not an apple or some carrots. Another diet **prohibited** all sugar and all **grains**. Eating no sugar made sense to Laila, but because she could not eat grains, not even rice or wheat bread, she did not have much **energy**. Each diet she began with new hope, because this diet would be the one that fixed her. This diet would make people like her, make boys want to talk to her, make her thin, and make her life perfect. This diet would make her fit in to the sparkly prom dress.

going on diets (exp) – auf Diät sein
spinach - Spinat
Raw - roh
cooked - gekocht
steamed - gedämpft
roasted - geröstet
stick with it (exp) – dabei bleiben
queasy - mulmig
strange - seltsam
specific - genau
cabbage - Kohl
grapefruit - Grapefruit
forbidden - verboten
prohibited - untersagt
grains - Getreide
energy - Energie

But each diet **failed**! The reasons for **failure** were **myriad**. Most of the diets left Laila feeling very hungry all of the time, and she did not have enough energy to pay attention in school or play with her dog. Some diets were too hard to follow. She could not **go out to eat** with her friends or buy lunch at school. Some diets **excluded** Laila's very favorite foods, and even when she **resisted** for weeks at a time, eventually she would give up and eat. The diets did not make Laila popular, and they did not make her thin. She felt like even more of a failure. Laila had good grades in school; she was good in many subjects; she loved to read; she liked to **bike**, play **softball** and go **swimming**; she loved her family and was a kind, caring girl. None of that seemed to matter so long as Laila was still fat. Laila hated herself, and hated her body. And so did everyone else, **apparently**!

failed - fehlschlagen
failure - Versagen
myriad - Myriaden
go out to eat (exp) – ausgehen zum essen
excluded – ausschließen
resisted - widerstehen
bike - Fahrrad
softball - Softball
swimming - Schwimmen
apparently - anscheinend

As Laila grew older, her body started to change. She stopped **craving** foods with lots of sugar and she stopped wanting many foods with too much **grease**. She grew taller and her body became less fat. The clothes in the store started to fit her, and her family stopped making comments about her size and about her food choices, but Laila still felt bad when she looked in the mirror. She found other things about herself that she did not like. Now that her body was the right size, it was the wrong shape, her skin was too **blotchy**, her arms were too short, her **forehead** was too big, or her hair was too **frizzy**. **No matter what** anyone said, Laila could always find something wrong with herself!

"Laila, you look so pretty," her mother said, but Laila did not feel pretty. Laila felt the same as she always had, even though she was no longer fat.

"Do you have a boyfriend yet?" her dad asked.

"No," Laila said **miserably**, "boys hate me because I'm ugly."

"You are not ugly! You are beautiful now. Boys should be **throwing themselves** at you!"

But the boys did not throw themselves at Laila, because she still disliked herself and people could **tell**.

craving - verlangen
grease - Fett
blotchy - fleckig
forehead - Stirn
frizzy - gekräuselt
No matter what (exp) – was auch immer (komme was wolle)
miserably - kläglich
throwing themselves (exp) – sich auf dich schmeißen
tell - sagen

"I'll bet you are the most popular girl in school," Laila's grandmother said, but Laila had fewer friends now than ever because her **self-esteem** was so low. She felt ugly. She felt **worthless**. In fact, she felt worse than she did when she was fat! Because, now that she was not fat people treated her differently, but **losing weight** did not fix her heart.

self-esteem – Selbtachtung
worthless – wertlos
losing weight (exp) - abnehmen

One day, Laila was **walking her dog**. It was one of her favorite things to do. It was a beautiful spring day. The sky was the perfect shade of blue, **studded** with soft white clouds **here and there**. The temperature was perfect too, warm enough to wear a tee shirt, but not hot, with a **slight**, **refreshing breeze**. The spring rain had brought a **flush** of bright green **growth** to all the plants and trees, but today it was sunny, and everything looked so **vibrant**. Flowers were **blooming** everywhere, and she caught the soft **scents** of **honeysuckle** and **roses**. As she walked, Laila saw **butterflies** and chubby little **bumblebees**. The breeze **stirred** the grass. Her dog walked happily ahead of her with his cute little ears **bobbing** up and down and his pink tongue **hanging** out. In that moment, Laila was so happy just to be alive, that she forgot for a minute that she didn't like herself.

walking her dog (exp) – mit dem Hund rausgehen
studded - übersät
here and there (exp) – hier und da
slight - leichte
refreshing breeze – frische Briese
flush - Spülung
growth - Wachstum
vibrant - dynamisch
blooming - blühen
scents - Gerüche
honeysuckle - Geißblatt
roses - Rosen
butterflies - Schmetterlinge
bumblebees - Hummeln
stirred - rührte
bobbing - wippen
hanging - hängen

When the walk was over, Laila **realized** what had happened. As she filled her dog›s water bowl, Laila felt **grateful** that she could take her dog for walks. She felt good that she could fill his water bowl, give him a **biscuit** and tell him he was a good boy, and he would **wag** his tail and **nuzzle** her hand. And her dog didn›t care how she looked! Her dog **didn›t mind** what her skin or hair looked like. Laila›s dog loved her **no matter what**. Since her dog loved her, Laila began to wonder if it was **possible** for her to love herself.

realized - realisiert
grateful - dankbar
biscuit - Keks
wag - wackeln
nuzzle - schnüffeln
didn›t mind (exp) – war egal

no matter what (exp) – in jedem Fall
possible - möglich

With new **determination**, Laila decided that she would love herself, no matter what, just like her dog. If a dog could do it, surely she could! Even though she still had to buy the biggest size on the rack at the store. Even though her skin was not perfect. Even though her hair was wild and **disobedient**. But she did not know how to get started! All her life, people had told her she was not **lovable**, and she did not know how to change it.

determination - Entschlossenheit
disobedient - ungehorsam
lovable - liebenswert

First, she tried buying new clothes. She went with her friend to the store and looked at all of the pretty, sparkly clothes that never fit her when she was younger and fatter. She tried on **low-cut** shirts, short skirts, and **skinny jeans**. Some of the clothes were **uncomfortable** and made Laila feel very silly, but some of the clothes looked good! Laila bought herself a couple new outfits. She felt better with her new, stylish clothes, but she wasn't sure she loved herself yet.

low-cut - dekolletiert
skinny jeans – enge Jeans
uncomfortable - ungemütlich

Next, Laila went swimming without a t-shirt. All her life, she had worn a **baggy** t-shirt in the pool because she was so embarrassed about her body. So, she decided to go swimming without the cover-up. It was scary because Laila was afraid that people would make fun of her, or stare at her, even though she was much smaller than before. She walked out of the ladies' locker room in nothing but a **bathing suit** and **flip-flops**, and no one stared! No one **looked at her twice**. She **hunched** over at first to appear smaller, but soon Laila stood up straight and tall, and she had a nice, long swim. Once her swim was over, she felt better, but she still wasn't sure she loved herself yet.

baggy - weites
bathing suit - Badeanzug
flip-flops - Flipflops
looked at her twice (exp) – musste sie zweimal anschauen
hunched - krümmte

Next, Laila decided to dance. Her friends went to a **dance club** every couple of weeks and Laila had never been, because she was afraid that people would stare at her and **tease** her because of how she looked or how she danced. Laila **called up** one of her friends and asked if they were going out that night. They said they were, so Laila asked to come with them. Laila wore a short skirt and a cute top, and she took the time to put on makeup and do her hair. She was very, very nervous. She was **shaking** a little when she went into the club because she was so scared. But her friends **clustered** around her, **giggling** and **chatting**, and soon they were all out on the dance floor in a big group. Laila forgot how nervous she was and danced with her friends until very late at night. Laila **had a great time**, but she still wasn›t sure she loved herself yet.

dance club – Club
tease - necken
called up (exp) – rief her
shaking - zittern
clustered - gruppieren
giggling - kichern
chatting - unterhalten
had a great time (exp) – hatte eine tolle Zeit

Last, as part of her quest to love herself, Laila started looking in the mirror. She used to look in the mirror for just a **second**, just long enough to check her hair and outfit and then she would look away in **shame**. She started looking in the mirror for longer **periods** of time. Laila made eye contact with herself, and at first, it was **unnerving**. She felt **awkward** and uncomfortable, but she made herself stay, until she could stand in front of the mirror for minutes at a time. Then she practiced smiling at herself. It felt

stupid at first to **fake**-smile at herself in the mirror but, after she practiced it a few times, Laila found that she actually enjoyed smiling at herself! It felt good to see someone smile at her! And when she looked in the mirror and felt bad, Laila started telling herself, "It›s okay. I love you. You›re a good person." She did this every single day. Sometimes it felt stupid and sometimes it felt nice, but she still wasn›t sure she loved herself yet.

second - Sekunde
shame - Scham
periods - Periode
unnerving - zermürbend
awkward - seltsam
stupid - komisch
fake - falsch

After many months of practice, Laila woke up one day and realized that she loved herself, **unequivocally**: as much as she loved her parents, as much as she loved her grandma, and as much as she loved her dog. She realized that self-hate and self-love did not come from a **dress size** or a number on the **scale**. She had been fat and hated herself, and she had been thin and hated herself. It had nothing to do with size! Self-worth, Laila realized, was something that she had to **cultivate** within herself. It was a hard lesson to learn, but it was also the most **valuable** lesson Laila had ever learned. Once she had her self-worth and self-love, nothing and no one could ever take it from her again.

unequivocally - eindeutig
dress size - Kleidergröße
scale - Waage
cultivate - aufbauen
valuable - wertvoll

Vocabulary:

prom - Ball
sighed - seufzte
champagne-colored – champagnerfarbig
gauzy - hauchdünn
poofy - tuntenhaft
turquoise-colored – türkisfarbend
crystals – Glitzersteine
bust - Brust
admired - bewundert
plus size (exp) – XXL-Abteilung
sparkly - schimmernd
honey - Honig
business - Geschäft
blazer - Blazer
groaned - stöhnte
protested - protestierte
peruse - durchgehen
church - Kirche
olive green – olivgrün
embroidered - bestickt
neckline - Ausschnitt
sleeves - Ärmel
It›s okay (exp) – es ist okay
I guess (exp) – ich denke
grumbled - grummeln
embarrassed - peinlich
compromise - Kompromisse eingehen
chore - Aufgabe
exhausted - ermüdet
depressed - deprimiert
deserve - verdient
stylish – schick, modern
exclusively - exklusive
expensive - teuer
middle-aged divorcee – geschieden im mittleren Alter

made (exp) - gemacht
fun of her (exp) - ausgelacht
forced - gezwungen
meant well (exp) – gut gemeint
counter - entgegnen
starving - verhungern
dizzy - schwindelig
faint – Ohnmächtig werden
had a crush on (exp) – verliebt sein
Little did Laila know (exp) – aber Laila wusste nicht
liked her (exp) – mochte sie
going on diets (exp) – auf Diät sein
spinach - Spinat
Raw - roh
cooked - gekocht
steamed - gedämpft
roasted - geröstet
stick with it (exp) – dabei bleiben
queasy - mulmig
strange - seltsam
specific - genau
cabbage - Kohl
grapefruit - Grapefruit
forbidden - verboten
prohibited - untersagt
grains - Getreide
energy - Energie
failed - fehlschlagen
failure - Versagen
myriad - Myriaden
go out to eat (exp) – ausgehen zum essen
excluded – ausschließen
resisted - widerstehen
bike - Fahrrad
softball - Softball
swimming - Schwimmen
apparently - anscheinend
craving - verlangen

grease - Fett
blotchy - fleckig
forehead - Stirn
frizzy - gekräuselt
No matter what (exp) – was auch immer (komme was wolle)
miserably - kläglich
throwing themselves (exp) – sich auf dich schmeißen
tell - sagen
self-esteem – Selbtachtung
worthless – wertlos
losing weight (exp) - abnehmen
walking her dog (exp) – mit dem Hund rausgehen
studded - übersät
here and there (exp) – hier und da
slight - leichte
refreshing breeze – frische Briese
flush - Spülung
growth - Wachstum
vibrant - dynamisch
blooming - blühen
scents - Gerüche
honeysuckle - Geißblatt
roses - Rosen
butterflies - Schmetterlinge
bumblebees - Hummeln
stirred - rührte
bobbing - wippen
hanging - hängen
realized - realisiert
grateful - dankbar
biscuit - Keks
wag - wackeln
nuzzle - schnüffeln
didn›t mind (exp) – war egal
no matter what (exp) – in jedem Fall
possible - möglich
determination - Entschlossenheit
disobedient - ungehorsam

lovable - liebenswert
low-cut - dekolletiert
skinny jeans – enge Jeans
uncomfortable - ungemütlich
baggy - weites
bathing suit - Badeanzug
flip-flops - Flipflops
looked at her twice (exp) – musste sie zweimal anschauen
hunched - krümmte
dance club – Club
tease - necken
called up (exp) – rief her
shaking - zittern
clustered - gruppieren
giggling - kichern
chatting - unterhalten
had a great time (exp) – hatte eine tolle Zeit
second - Sekunde
shame - Scham
periods - Periode
unnerving - zermürbend
awkward - seltsam
stupid - komisch
fake - falsch
unequivocally - eindeutig
dress size - Kleidergröße
scale - Waage
cultivate - aufbauen
valuable - wertvoll

Muffin the Cat

Sometimes we **take for granted** the presence of animals in our lives, never stopping to think how they **shape** us as people. Have you ever had a pet that you loved very much? What happened to that pet? What is your **fondest** memory of that pet? Did you have other pets? What other **meaningful encounters** with animals can you think of?

take for granted (exp) – nicht zu schätzen wissen
shape - formen
fondest - liebevollste
meaningful - bedeutungsvoll
encounters - Begegnungen

Cats were Katie's favorite animal. She drew pictures of cats, read books about cats, and **recited** facts about cats at the dinner table.

"The **scientific** name for a cat is Felis catus," she said.

"That's nice," said Katie's mom.

"Cats have a **variable** number of **bones** in their **tail**," said Katie.

"Interesting," said Katie's dad.

recited - vortragen
scientific - wissenschaftlich
variable - unterschiedlich
bones - Knochen
tail - Schwanz

Katie had never **had a pet** before. On her fifth birthday, Katie's parents took her to the **county animal shelter**, because Katie wanted nothing in the entire world more than a pet kitten. **Rescuing** animals was important to Katie's family because, in many animal shelters, the animals were eventually **put to sleep** if they did not get **adopted**.

had a pet (exp) – hatte ein Haustier
county - Berirk
animal shelter - Tierheim
Rescuing - retten
were put to sleep (exp) - eingeschläfert
adopted - adoptiert

The shelter had a **strange** smell to it, because the animals were kept **indoors** and then the shelter **staff** had to clean up after them. Everything looked gray to Katie as she walked behind her mother. A lady who worked at the shelter led them through the shelter to the place where the cats were kept. Katie's mouth hung open as she stared at the metal **cages** that went from the floor to the **ceiling**. They had solid **stainless steel** bottoms and were built in to the wall, and perhaps two **dozen** cats occupied the cages. Katie wandered in front of the ones on the floor because they were closest to eye level, and she **admired** the beautiful cats inside. There was a big, **striped** orange cat **napping** on its bed. There was a small, **chubby**, white cat sitting in the corner. There was a brown cat making **chirping** noises as another visitor poked a **feathered** toy through the cage to play with it.

Strange - merkwürdig
indoors - Innen
staff - Angestellten
cages - Käfige
ceiling - Decke
stainless steel - Stahl
dozen - dutzend
admired - bewundert
striped - gestreift
napping - schlafen
chubby – dicker (wohlgenährt)

chirping - zirpend
feathered - gefiedert

All of the cats and kittens were so cute and friendly that Katie didn't know how she would ever choose. Then she looked up, and in one of the cages at the very top, sat a tiny black and white kitten with gold-green eyes. Katie and the kitten **locked** eyes, and a **ray** of sun coming through the window made the kitten's eyes **sparkle**.

Locked - fixieren, in die Augen schauen
ray - Strahl
sparkle - funkeln

"That one!" Katie **cried**, pointing to the kitten. "Let's take her home!"

"You have to meet her first," Katie's mother said.

The lady who worked for the shelter opened the kitten's cage and carried the kitten to a small room where people could meet the animals they wanted to adopt. Katie could **hardly** contain her **excitement** as the shelter worker placed the little black and white kitten on the floor. Katie **approached** the kitten and **squatted** down beside to **pet** her very carefully.

"She's so soft," Katie observed, "she's perfect! I want *her*!"

"Okay," said Katie's mother, "**we'll take her**!"

Muffin (that was the kitten's name) was quiet for the whole ride home. She rode in a **cardboard** box with air holes in the side, sitting on Katie's lap.

cried - schrie
hardly -kaum
excitement - Aufregung
approached - näherte

squatted - hockte
pet - Haustier
we'll take her (exp) - Wir nehmen Sie!
cardboard - Karton

When they got back to the house, Muffin came out of the box and started **exploring immediately**. Katie fed her some **treats** and wanted to pet her some more, but Muffin had other ideas! She ran around with all the **energy** of a small kitten, **diving** under **furniture**, sticking her head in **cabinets**, and jumping up on counter tops. She even climbed on top of the **refrigerator**! Katie was **disappointed** that Muffin did not want to play, so she went to her room to play by herself. She sat down to play with her dolls, but a few minutes later, Muffin came running into the room and **attacked** the doll's hair! Katie giggled and **shrieked** as Muffin **clamped** down on the doll's head with her **paws**, and they became best friends.

Exploring - umsehen
immediately - sofort
treats -Leckereien
energy - Energie
diving - springen
furniture - Möbel
cabinets - Schränke
refrigerator - Kühlschrank
disappointed - enttäuscht
attacked - attakierte
shrieked - schreite
clamped -klemmte
paws - Pfoten

Katie played dolls with Muffin every day after that, and her dolls **took a beating**, but Katie did not mind. She was happy to share them with her friend. Katie loved to read, and whenever she sat down to read, Muffin would find her and sit in her lap. Muffin was there when she watched **cartoons**, and Muffin begged for food at **mealtimes**. Katie **sneaked** bits of meat to Muffin under the table. Katie wrote songs and poems and stories about Muffin because she loved her so much.

took a beating (exp) – sahen abgenutzt aus
cartoons - Zeichentrickserien
mealtimes - Essenszeiten
sneaked - schmuggelte

Sometimes Muffin **misbehaved**, because she was a small kitten. She knocked over cups full of water or milk, she **clawed** the furniture, and she attacked the feet of sleeping parents in the middle of the night. Katie's dad would get mad and yell at the kitten, and Katie thought it was funny, even though she did not like it that her dad was yelling at her friend.

misbehaved – schlecht benommen
clawed - zerkratzte

Katie and Muffin lived together for a few months before Katie's parents started **fighting** a lot. Her dad stopped yelling at Muffin because he was angry with her mom, and Katie's mom was angry at her dad. Katie did not understand what was going on! Why was everyone so angry all the time? No one **bothered** to explain it to Katie, and she was **frightened**. Muffin stayed with her through those scary nights, laying beside Katie in bed and **purring** to help put her to sleep.

Fighting - streiten
bothered - kümmert
frightened - verängstigt
purring - schnurren

Soon after that, Katie's dad **moved out**. Katie did not understand why. She felt very sad, and her mom explained that Katie's dad had to live somewhere else because they were **getting a divorce**.

Muffin the Cat

"What is a **divorce**?" Katie asked Muffin, because Katie's mom was angry these days and Katie was afraid to ask her. Muffin only looked at Katie.

"Is a divorce very big? Is that why Daddy has to leave, to make room for it?" Muffin did not have the answer to this question, either.

"Is a divorce a different type of dad?" Katie asked. Muffin blinked, just once, very slowly.

"Maybe it's a different kind of house where Daddy will go live now." This thought made Katie very sad. She did not want her dad to leave. She cried a little bit, and Muffin sat in her lap, **licking** Katie's hand.

Katie cried a lot more when she realized her dad truly was not going to live there anymore. She learned that she would only get to see her dad once or twice a week, and she cried even more. Katie still didn't understand what a divorce was, but she knew that she really, really **hated** it.

moved out (exp) - ausgezogen war
getting a divorce (exp) – sich scheiden lassen
divorce - Scheidung
licking - lecken
hated - hasste

Eventually, she **got used to** her dad not being around, although she still missed him, and his **absence** made her heart hurt. Having Muffin there to **cuddle** with her helped Katie feel a tiny bit better, though.

Katie **got older** and started school. She did not have as much time for Muffin, but Muffin **did not seem to mind**. They were still best friends, and Muffin still slept on Katie's bed every night. Katie still drew pictures of Muffin, and she still wrote stories and poems about her. Katie made friends at school, and she was no longer sure that Muffin was her best friend, but Muffin did not seem to mind that either.

got used to (exp) – hat sich dran gewöhnt
absence - Abwesenheit
cuddle - kuscheln
got older (exp) – wurde älter
did not seem to mind (exp) – störte es nicht

When Katie entered **high school**, Muffin was pretty old, for a cat. Some of the black fur on her face had turned white. She did not **scamper** and play as much as she used to. She slept a lot more. Katie knew that her friend was getting older, and it was hard to watch. Eventually, Muffin got very **sick**, and was in a lot of pain, and could hardly move. Katie hated to see her friend like this. Soon, Muffin was put to sleep to end her **suffering**.

high school - Oberschule
scamper -flitzen
sick - krank
suffering - leiden

Katie cried and cried, because Muffin was her best friend for such a long time. Muffin helped her through so many hard things in life. Who would sleep on her feet and keep them warm in the **winter time**, Katie wondered? Who would sit on her lap while she did her homework? Who would lick her face to wake her up in the mornings? Who would be there to cuddle when Katie was having a bad day? Katie was going to **miss** Muffin very, very much. She hung a picture of Muffin on her bedroom wall so that she would remember her friend **forever**.

Time went by. She never forgot Muffin, but Katie felt less and less sad every time she looked at Muffin's picture on the wall. In time, Katie smiled when she looked at Muffin's picture, because she had so many **fond memories** of Muffin the cat.

winter time – Winterzeit
miss - vermissen
forever – Für immer
fond memories -liebevolle Erinnerungen

A few months after Muffin **passed on**, Katie and her mom got a dog. The dog was adopted from the shelter too. He was not a young puppy but a three-year-old **adult** dog. His name was Sargent, but everyone called him Sarge for short. He was a big, brown and black dog, with **floppy** ears and **beady** brown eyes. His favorite game in the world was **fetch**, and he loved to go on long, long walks with Katie when she came home from school. Katie had never had a dog before, so it was hard at first **to get to know** Sarge.

passed on – verstorben war
adult - erwachsen
floppy - schlapp
beady - perlend
fetch - fangen
to get to know - kennenlernen

One day, Katie's **boyfriend broke up with her**. Katie was **heartbroken**. She cried all day at school, then came home and cried some more. She laid down on her bed and **curled up** tight, **hugging** her **knees** to her **chest**. Katie cried even harder when she **realized** that Muffin would not come sit with her this time! Katie felt very **alone**.

boyfriend – Freund (Beziehung)
broke up with her (exp) – Schluss gemacht
heartbroken – untröstlich
curled up (exp) - eingekringelt
hugging - umarmen
knees - Knie
chest - Brust
realized - realisiert
alone - alleine

But just a few minutes after she lay down, Katie heard a sound in her room. Then something cold and wet **pressed** into the back of her **neck**! She sat up, **startled**, and there was Sarge, sitting by her bed, staring up at her with his beady brown eyes, and Katie could not be sure but she thought the dog looked **worried** about her, with his dog **eyebrows** raised. Even though Sarge was a grown dog, he was very cute. Katie had to smile. Sarge **nuzzled** her knee, and Katie petted his head, then she **invited** him to sit on the bed with her. Sarge happily **obliged**, and Katie hugged his neck and she **sniffled** and cried a little more into Sarge's **fur**.

Pressed - drückte
neck - Nacken
startled - erschrocken
worried - sorgen
eyebrows - Augenbrauen
nuzzled - beschnüffelte
invited - eingeladen
obliged - verpflichtet
sniffled - schniefte
fur - Fell

"Why did Bobby break up with me?" Katie asked Sarge. Sarge **grunted** in response.

"He said he loved me!" she added, "Why does it have to be this way?" But Sarge did not have an answer for her.

"When will it stop hurting? When will I meet another boy like him? Will anyone else ever want me to be their **girlfriend**? Will I stop missing him?" Sarge couldn't answer those questions either, so he **patiently** licked Katie's **elbow**. Katie missed Muffin and she was sad about her boyfriend, but Sarge helped her feel a whole lot better.

grunted - murrte
girlfriend – Freundin (Beziehung)
patiently - geduldig
elbow - Ellebogen

Ten years later, Katie **graduated college** with a **degree in fine art**. She had a good **career** as a **photographer**, and now she had her **very own** photography **business**. Her specialties were **wedding** photos and pet **portraits**. Katie loved photographing people's pets, so that they would have a nice photo to remember them by forever. Katie was also **engaged** to be married to a good, **handsome** man named Ali. Ali was training to be a **nurse** at the hospital. Katie visited her mom every week. Sarge still lived with Katie's mom, and Katie lived with her fiancé. Even though she did not see Sarge as often, Katie still took him on walks. Sometimes, she still told him her **troubles**, and Sarge still listened to her and patiently licked her elbow. But Katie could see that Sarge was getting older.

graduated college – absolvierte die Hochschule
degree in fine art - Abschluss in Kunst
career - Karriere
photographer - Fotografin
very own (exp) - eigenes
business - Geschäft
wedding - Hochzeit
portraits - Porträts
engaged - verlobt
handsome – gutaussehend
nurse - Krankenschwester
troubles - Schwierigkeiten

One day, Katie's mom called and said that Sarge had **passed away** in his sleep, and Katie was very sad. She was going to miss Sarge, maybe even more than she missed Muffin!

Katie and her fiancé did not get another pet after Sarge died for a long, long time. They got married and **went on a honeymoon** to the Caribbean, then came back. Katie was **running her own business** as a photographer, and she was very busy; her husband was now working as a nurse, and he was very busy. Neither of them felt that they had the time to take good care of a pet.

Eight years later, Katie had a four-year-old **daughter**. When she asked her daughter, Nina, what she wanted for her fifth birthday, Nina **surprised** Katie by saying that she wanted a pet kitten! Nina did not have the same **fascination** for cats that Katie did at that age, but it was **natural** for a young kid to want a pet.

passed away (exp) - verstorben
went on a honeymoon (exp) – in den Flitterwochen
running her own business (exp) – hatte ihr eigenes Geschäft
daughter - Tochter
surprised - überrascht
fascination - Faszination
natural - natürlich

Katie fondly remembered her fifth birthday, when her mother took her to the shelter and she met Muffin. She remembered how much it hurt when Muffin was put to sleep, but she also remembered how many long years of happiness and **friendship** she and Muffin shared. Muffin was such a good **companion** while she was growing up. Katie and her husband were still very busy, but they agreed that Nina could have a kitten of her very own.

Katie took her daughter to the animal shelter on her fifth birthday, and she was **gobsmacked** to see, sitting placidly in one of the cages on top, a tiny black and white kitten with gold-green eyes. He looked just like Muffin! Katie didn't say anything, she wanted Nina to make the **decision**, but she had to smile when Nina saw the black-and-white kitten and pointed at it **excitedly**.

friendship - Freundschaft
companion - Begleiter
gobsmacked - baff
decision - Entscheidung
excitedly - aufgeregt

"That one! I want him! He's so cute, Mommy!" Nina cried.

"You have to meet him first," Katie laughed.

Muffin the Cat

"Okay!" Nina said, as the shelter worker opened the cage and lifted the little black-and-white kitten out of the cage. They went to the visiting room and Nina played with the kitten for a few minutes. "He's perfect!"

"What will you name him?" the shelter worker asked.

Nina **considered**, then said **proudly**, "His name is Muffin."

considered - überlegte
proudly - stolz

Vocabulary:

take for granted (exp) – nicht zu schätzen wissen
shape - formen
fondest - liebevollste
meaningful - bedeutungsvoll
encounters - Begegnungen
recited - vortragen
scientific - wissenschaftlich
variable - unterschiedlich
bones - Knochen
tail - Schwanz
had a pet (exp) – hatte ein Haustier
county - Berirk
animal shelter - Tierheim
Rescuing - retten
were put to sleep (exp) - eingeschläfert
adopted - adoptiert
Strange - merkwürdig
indoors - Innen
staff - Angestellten
cages - Käfige
ceiling - Decke
stainless steel - Stahl
dozen - dutzend
admired - bewundert
striped - gestreift
napping - schlafen
chubby – dicker (wohlgenährt)
chirping - zirpend
feathered - gefiedert
Locked - fixieren, in die Augen schauen
ray - Strahl
sparkle - funkeln
cried - schrie
hardly -kaum
excitement - Aufregung

approached - näherte
squatted - hockte
pet - Haustier
we'll take her (exp) - Wir nehmen Sie!
cardboard - Karton
Exploring - umsehen
immediately - sofort
treats -Leckereien
energy - Energie
diving - springen
furniture - Möbel
cabinets - Schränke
refrigerator - Kühlschrank
disappointed - enttäuscht
attacked - attakierte
shrieked - schreite
clamped -klemmte
paws - Pfoten
took a beating (exp) – sahen abgenutzt aus
cartoons - Zeichentrickserien
mealtimes - Essenszeiten
sneaked - schmuggelte
misbehaved – schlecht benommen
clawed - zerkratzte
Fighting - streiten
bothered - kümmert
frightened - verängstigt
purring - schnurren
moved out (exp) - ausgezogen war
getting a divorce (exp) – sich scheiden lassen
divorce - Scheidung
licking - lecken
hated - hasste
got used to (exp) – hat sich dran gewöhnt
absence - Abwesenheit
cuddle - kuscheln
got older (exp) – wurde älter
did not seem to mind (exp) – störte es nicht

high school - Oberschule
scamper -flitzen
sick - krank
suffering - leiden
winter time – Winterzeit
miss - vermissen
forever – Für immer
fond memories -liebevolle Erinnerungen
passed on – verstorben war
adult - erwachsen
floppy - schlapp
beady - perlend
fetch - fangen
to get to know - kennenlernen
boyfriend – Freund (Beziehung)
broke up with her (exp) – Schluss gemacht
heartbroken – untröstlich
curled up (exp) - eingekringelt
hugging - umarmen
knees - Knie
chest - Brust
realized - realisiert
alone - alleine
Pressed - drückte
neck - Nacken
startled - erschrocken
worried - sorgen
eyebrows - Augenbrauen
nuzzled - beschnüffelte
invited - eingeladen
obliged - verpflichtet
sniffled - schniefte
fur - Fell
grunted - murrte
girlfriend – Freundin (Beziehung)
patiently - geduldig
elbow - Ellebogen
graduated college – absolvierte die Hochschule

degree in fine art - Abschluss in Kunst
career - Karriere
photographer - Fotografin
very own (exp) - eigenes
business - Geschäft
wedding - Hochzeit
portraits - Porträts
engaged - verlobt
handsome – gutaussehend
nurse - Krankenschwester
troubles - Schwierigkeiten
passed away (exp) - verstorben
went on a honeymoon (exp) – in den Flitterwochen
running her own business (exp) – hatte ihr eigenes Geschäft
daughter - Tochter
surprised - überrascht
fascination - Faszination
natural - natürlich
friendship - Freundschaft
companion - Begleiter
gobsmacked - baff
decision - Entscheidung
excitedly - aufgeregt
considered - überlegte
proudly - stolz

Someday a Chef

Tucker's mom did not like to cook when he was **growing up**. Even at a young age, Tucker **accepted** this fact. Some people like to cook, some people do not, he **reasoned**. Tucker's mom liked to do other things, like **sewing**, **writing**, and watching **sci-fi**, but she did not like to cook!

growing up - erwachsen wude
accepted - akzeptieren
reasoned - begründet
sewing - Nähen
writing - Schreiben
sci-fi - Science-Fiction

Consequently, Tucker's family did not eat very well, or very **adventurously**. A "**fancy**" meal in Tucker's family consisted of **spaghetti** and a jar of **sauce**, and sometimes, if they were having **company**, a fresh **baguette** or bag of **salad**. Many nights, dinner came from a **can**, a **box**, or a **jar**. **Frozen pizza** was a **household staple**. **Rarely** did they eat **vegetables**. Many other nights, dinner came through the **window** of a **fast food drive-through**. Tucker's favorite was **hamburgers**. He liked to eat, he **appreciated** the taste of food, but deep down inside, he knew that something was **missing**.

consequently - folglich
adventurously - sonderlich
fancy - schick
spaghetti - Spaghetti
sauce - Soße
baguette - Baguette
salad - Salat
having company (exp) - Besuch
can - Dose
box - Box

jar - Glas
Frozen pizza - Tiefkühlpizza
household staple – Grundnahrungsmittel im Haushalt
Rarely - Selten
vegetables - Gemüse
window - Fenster
fast food – Fastfood
drive-through (exp) - Durchfahrtsbedienung
hamburgers - Hamburger
appreciated - dankbar
missing - fehlt

It was in this **culinary wasteland** that Tucker was **born and raised**. He really enjoyed eating, but was never **exposed** to different types of cooking until he made friends with a Korean boy, David, in the **sixth grade**. David invited Tucker to his house for **sleepovers**. During those sleepovers, David›s mom ordered **pizza**, because she wanted Tucker to feel at home, and was **worried** that Tucker would not like Korean food.

culinary wasteland – Kulinarische Einöde
born and raised (exp) - aufgewachsen
exposed - vertraut gemacht
sixth grade – sechste Klasse
sleepovers - Übernachtungen
pizza - Pizza
worried – sorgen machen

"Do you guys always eat pizza?" Tucker asked, because he had seen different kinds of food when passing through David's kitchen, and when David opened the **refrigerator** to get a **soda**.

"No! Mom only gets pizza when you're here," David **admitted**. "She thinks you won't like Korean food."

"I would love to try it!" Tucker **exclaimed**. "**How else** will I know if I like it or not?"

After that **conversation** with David, Tucker got to try new and exciting foods like home-made **ramen** with **boiled eggs**, **dduk-bokki**, **bibimbap**, **jajangmyeon**, and **fried rice** with **kimchi**. His favorite Korean meal was **jajangmyeon** for dinner with **gyeo-ngju** bread for **dessert**. Tucker loved every new food he tried, and because of these meals shared with David, he would one day **embark** on a **magical culinary journey**.

refrigerator - Kühlschrank
soda - Limonade
admitted - zugegeben
exclaimed - rief
How else (exp) - wie sonst
conversation - Unterhaltung
ramen – Ramen Nudeln
boiled eggs – gekochte Eier
ddukbokki – Koreanisches Essen
bibimbap – Koreanisches Essen
jajangmyeon – Koreanisches Essen
fried rice – gebratener Reis
kimchi – Koreanisches Essen
jajangmyeon – Koreanisches Essen
gyeongju – Koreanisches Essen
dessert - Nachspeise
embark - einsteigen
magical culinary journey – magische kulinarische Reise

Tucker did not realize that he could have made these foods at home for himself. He had never seen anyone **devote** time and **energy** to making food, so it never **entered** his mind that he could make and enjoy different types of food. In his mind, David's family was just different, and there was no way that Tucker could ever be like them and make delicious food like that. At home, Tucker and his family still ate **packaged** food and hamburgers, but Tuck-er had started watching **cooking shows**, **longing** for a better food life. At first, he only watched **reality** shows where people **competed** to **build** the **tallest sugar sculpture** or the **craziest** looking **cake** or make a five **course** meal the **fastest**. But soon he became interested in other types of shows. Tucker started watching normal cooking shows, where the host **demonstrates** how to **prepare** a dish or meal. He was **absolutely fascinated**. Tucker had never seen someone carefully **slicing carrots** like that, making sure they were just the right **thickness** so they would have just the right **texture** when cooked. His eyes went wide as he watched an American chef lovinglydice an **onion** and then **caramelize** it in a **skillet** full of hot **oil**. He grinned until his face hurt as he watched an Italian chef mix **dough** for **fresh pasta** with her **bare hands** - he thought pasta could only come out of a box! He sighed with **longing** as he watched a French chef make a perfect **roux** with as much **grace** and **ease** as **breathing**. These people treated their food with such **tender** care, there were so many **colors**, and it all looked so **delicious**!

Devote - widmen
energy - Energie
entered - eintreten
packaged - verpackt
cooking shows – Kochsendungen
longing - Sehnsucht
reality - Realität
competed - konkurriert
build - bauen
tallest - höchste
sugar sculpture – Zuckerskulptur
craziest - verrückteste
cake - Kuchen
course - Gang
fastest - schnellste
demonstrates - vorstellt
prepare - vorbereiten
absolutely fascinated – total fasziniert
slicing carrots – Karotten schneiden
thickness - Dicke
texture - Konsistenz
lovingly dice – liebevoll stückeln

onion - Zwiebel
caramelize - Karamellisieren
skillet -Bratpfanne
oil - Öl
dough - Teig
fresh pasta – frische Nudeln
bare hands – blanke Hände
longing - sehnsüchtig
roux - Mehlschwitze
grace - Anmut
ease - Leichtigkeit
breathing - atmen
tender - zart
colors - Farben
delicious - köstlich

Tucker **was in love**.

For a long time, he just watched the cooking shows, but he watched them **voraciously**. Every **spare** hour he devoted to watching these **masters** of the kitchen **practice** their **craft**. He longed to do what they did, but he was **afraid**. What if he started an oil **fire** while trying to fry onions? What if he mixed the pasta dough wrong and **wasted** all that flour? What if he **burnt** the roux? Better to leave the cooking to the people who knew what they were doing and just watch from a safe **distance**. If he tried to cook and **messed it up**, his mom might get angry with him.

was in love (exp) - verliebt
voraciously - heißhungrig
spare -freie
masters -Profis
practice - ausüben
craft - Handwerk
afraid - angst
fire - Feuer
wasted - verschwendet
burnt -verbrannt

distance -Abstand
messed it up (exp) - vermasselt

Finally, when Tucker went away to **college**, he got his very own **apartment** near **campus**. It was a small place but **comfortable** enough for one person, and the best part - it had a **kitchen**! The kitchen was **equipped** with all **brand-new appliances**: it had a big metal **sink** with deep sides; a refrigerator with a **spacious freezer**; and a **stove** with a flat, **ceramic glass electric cooktop**. **Finally**, it was Tucker's turn to make choices about what happened in the kitchen! When he went shopping, he had a choice between a box of dry pasta or some flour and eggs to make fresh pasta. He had a choice between a frozen pizza or fresh meat and vegetables. He had a choice between buying a loaf of sad, white bread **packed** full of **preservatives** and trying to bake his own bread.

college - Hochschule
apartment - Wohnung
campus - Universitätsgelände
comfortable - gemütlich
kitchen - Küche
equipped - ausgestattet
brand-new appliances – neue Geräte
sink - Spüle
spacious freezer – geräumige Gefriertruhe
stove - Herd
ceramic glass electric cook top - Cerankochfeld
Finally - endlich
packed - eingepackt
preservatives - Konservierungsstoffe

The first **dish** Tucker tried to make was his very own jajangmyeon. He went to the store and **carefully** selected all the **ingredients**, choosing the very best-looking vegetables, and the freshest **mincedpork**. He found a **packet** of fresh **noodles**, and they even had **mirin**! The only ingredient missing now was the **black bean paste**, which David had called **chunjang**. That was the key to jajangmyeon: it just wouldn't be jajangmyeon without it! Tucker had to find a special grocery store that **carried** Asian foods. Then he spent a long time walking around, with his mouth hanging open **in awe** of all **the** interesting and new foods he saw. They had vegetables here that Tucker had never seen. They had different types of bread, different noodles, and some things that Tucker did not even **recognize** - nor could he read the package because Tucker did not know Korean! It took a long time to find the chunjang, but soon Tucker was on the way home with all the ingredients for jajangmyeon. It was going to be the best jajang-myeon ever!

dish - Gericht
carefully - sorgfältig
ingredients - Zutaten
minced pork – gehacktes Schwein
packet - Packung
noodles - Nudeln
mirin - Reiswein
black bean paste – Schwarze Bohnenpaste
chunjang – Schwarze Bohnenpaste (koreanisch)
carried - beinhalten
in awe - bewundernd
recognize - erinnern

Tucker read the **recipe** and got started. He chopped the vegetables carefully, making sure they were all the right size pieces. He heated the oil before adding the **meat**, but the oil started to **smoke**! It smelled **awful**! Tucker turned **down** the heat and the oil stopped smoking. He added the meat to the pan, but now the oil was not hot enough, it took a long time for it to cook all the way through, and it was not **crispy** like the recipe said. Then he added the vegetables, but he did not read the recipe **closely**, and he **accidentally** added all the vegetables at the same time! The **onion** and the **zucchini** burned while the **potato** and the **radish** **stayed** too **hard**. He forgot to fry the **bean paste** in oil in the middle of the pan, so he just **stirred** it in and added some water. While the sauce was cooking, he cooked the noodles too. When the noodles were done, he drained them, piled them in a big bowl and poured lots of sauce on top. He took a **bite**, and... **yuck**! It tasted **terrible**! Tucker felt **discouraged**, because he had worked so hard to make a great jajangmyeon, and he had failed. He sat down to watch one of his favorite cooking shows, and the chef on television said, "If there are any **beginner** chefs out there, just remember, it takes a long time to learn to cook well. Start simple, and **work your way up**." So Tucker wondered if he had not started **simply** enough. By the time the show ended, Tucker's **resolve** was **renewed**, and he was **determined** to learn how to cook really, really well.

recipe - Rezept
meat - Fleisch
smoke - qualmen
awful - furchtbar
down - runterschalten
crispy - knusprig
closely - genau
accidentally - ausversehen
onion - Zwiebel
zucchini - Zuccini
potato - Kartoffel
radish stayed – Rettich blieb
hard - hart
bean paste – Bohnenpaste
stirred - rührte
bite - Biss
yuck - Pfui
terrible - furchtbar
discouraged - entmutigt
beginner - Anfänger
work your way up (exp) - Hocharbeiten
simply - einfach
resolve - lösen
renewed - erneuern
determined - entschlossen

Tucker started over again with simple stir-fries. It was hard to mess up a **stir-fry** and there were as many ways to make a stir-fry as one could imagine! Tucker could use **chicken**, or **shrimp**, or **tofu**; he could use **snap peas**, or **broccoli**, or a mix of **bell peppers**; he could make it **dry**, he could make a **sauce**, or he could mix in an egg. For **weeks**, all Tucker did was make stir-fries and teach himself how to chop vegetables, how to cook meat, and how to make the perfect pot of rice. Then, slowly, Tucker started **experimenting** with other types of cooking. He learned how to **sauté**, and how to **roast**. He had a friend who owned a **charcoal grill**, so he learned how to **grill** food, too! He was **cautious**, because Tucker felt like if he made a mistake, he would be **disrespecting** all the masters on television who had shown him the way. He made many **mistakes**, as everyone does when they are learning a new **skill**, but he learned from every mistake and ate a lot more of his own bad cooking: stir-fries with sauce so **thick** it **resembled jelly**, pans of burnt onions, and dishes so **salty** that it made his eyes **water**.

stir-fry - gebratenes
chicken - Hähnchen
shrimp - Schrimps
tofu - Tofu
snap peas - Erbsen
broccoli - Broccoli
bell peppers - Paprika
dry - trocken
sauce - Soße
weeks - Wochen
experimenting - experimentieren
saute - anbraten
roast - rösten
charcoal grill - Kohlegrill
grill - grillen
cautious - aufmerksam
disrespecting - Nichtachtung
mistakes - Fehler
skill - Fähigkeit

thick - dick
resembled jelly – ähnelt Wackelpudding
salty - salzig
water - Wasser

But Tucker got better and better. He even started to **dabble** in **baking**. He had always **admired** the people he saw baking on television. He was **amazed** by the amount of time, **effort**, and **detail** that the **pastry chefs** put into their **desserts**, which would be **destroyed** and eaten in a matter of minutes. Tucker **calculated** that some desserts involved **hours** and hours' worth of work per **portion**! Tucker never reached the **level** of **patience** required to **pipe** an **intricate pattern** with **royal icing** on four dozen **sugar cookies**, but he did teach himself how to make an **excellent chocolate cake**, and he did learn how to make flower-shaped **decorations** out of **butter cream frosting**.

Dabble - sich versuchen
baking - Backen
admired - bewundern
amazed - begeistert
effort - anstrengung
detail - Detail
pastry chefs – Konditormeister
desserts - Nachtisch
destroyed - vernichtet
calculated - gerechnet
hours - Stunden
portion - Servierung
level - Grad
patience - Geduld
pipe - pumpen
intricate pattern – kompliziertes Muster
royal icing – königliche Zuckerglasur
sugar cookies - Kekse
excellent chocolate cake – hervorragender Schokoladen-kuchen

decorations - Dekorationen
buttercream frosting – Buttercreme Glasur

Tucker Tucker became known among his friends at college for his skills in cooking and baking. He threw **dinner parties**, he baked for friends' birthdays, and he became **famous** at **potlucks**. He even learned how to make a really delicious jajangmyeon (although it never tasted as good as David's).

dinner parties – Abendessen
famous - berühmt
potlucks – Essen bei dem jeder etwas mitbringt

Cooking and baking became Tucker's **obsession**. He got a job at a **restaurant** as a **prep cook**, and for months, all they would let him do was cut vegetables, meat and sometimes fruit. Eight, ten, twelve hours a day, Tucker **sliced** and **chopped** and **crushed**, until his feet were sore and his hands were tired, but he loved it. He loved everything to do with food, even if all he did was chop carrots. Tucker **was a happy camper**.

obsession - Besessenheit
restaurant - Restaurant
prep cook - Hilfskoch
sliced – in Scheiben geschnitten
chopped - zerhackt
crushed - zerdrückt
was a happy camper (exp) – war glücklich und zufrieden

One day, the **sous-chef** of the restaurant **called out**. His **wife** was having a **baby**! It was very exciting, but that meant that there was no sous-chef that day. The **chef appointed** Tucker as the sous-chef's **replacement**, just for the day, until they could find someone else **to pitch in**. The restaurant was very busy that night, but Tucker had spent the last year **absorbing** every **detail** about the **operation** of the kitchen, and **although** he was **nervous**, he knew he could do it.

sous-chef – stellvertretender Küchenchef
called out (exp) - rief
wife - Ehefrau
baby - Baby
chef appointed – Chef ernannte
replacement - Ersatz
to pitch in (exp) - einspringt
absorbing - absorbieren
detail - Detail
operation - Tätigkeit
although - obwohl
nervous - nervös

Orders came in **left and right**, the chef **barked** orders, everyone was working hard, and it was hot in the kitchen! It was especially hot where Tucker stood, right in front of the stove, **instructing** his prep cooks in a **confident** voice. He told them what they needed to do, what ingredients to prepare, and what **tools** were needed. Tucker **fried**, **sauteed**, **mixed**, **chopped**, **seasoned**, and **tasted**, and the night **flew by** in a whirl. He started working at three that **afternoon**, and they sent out the last order around **midnight**. Tucker could have **sworn** it had only been a few minutes, he had **had such a good time**!

Orders - Bestellungen
left and right (exp) – links und rechts
barked - bellten
instructing - anweisen
confident - selbstbewussten
tools - Werkzeug
fried - frittiert
sauteed - bratete an
mixed - verrührte
chopped - schnitt
seasoned - würzte
tasted - probierte
flew by (exp) – verging wie im Fluge
afternoon - Nachmittag

midnight - Mitternacht
sworn - geschworen
had such a good time (exp) – so eine gute Zeit

"You did a very good job tonight, Tucker," said the chef.

"Thank you, chef," Tucker said shyly. He really **looked up to** the chef and admired his work. It felt good to be **praised** by someone he **respected** so much.

"Thank you for **stepping in** for us. You did such a good job tonight, I'd like to offer you a more **permanent position** as sous-chef."

"Really?" Tucker grinned at the chef. "That would be **awesome**! I would love to! But what about the old sous-chef?"

"He's looking to **transfer** to a different restaurant to spend more time with his wife and the new baby," the chef explained. "Starting tomorrow, you're our new sous-chef!"

"Wow!"

"Congratulations, Tucker."

"Thank you, chef."

looked up to (exp) – Vorbild (jemanden bewundern)
praised - lobte
respected - respektiert
stepping in - eingesprungen
permanent position – permanente Position
awesome - hervorragend
transfer - versetzen

For the next four years, Tucker worked **tirelessly** as a sous-chef. He stayed in school but changed his major to **business**. He knew **with every fiber of his being** that he wanted to be in the food **in-**

dustry for the rest of his life, and he wanted one day to open his own restaurant. He **adored** food; he loved the **bustle** and noise of the kitchen on a busy night; and every night was a busy night.

tirelessly - unermüdlich
business - Themenbereich
with every fiber of his being (exp) – mit jeder Faser seines Körpers
industry - Branche
adored - bewunderte
bustle - Rummel

Eventually, the day came when Tucker got tired of being sous-chef. He wanted to design his own **menus** and make his own food, and while the chef at his **current job** was **supportive** of Tucker, he did not like to let others **make the calls** in his kitchen. Tucker looked and looked for an **opening** somewhere as head chef, but the industry was **extremely competitive**. Tucker was still so **young**, he had very little **experience by comparison**, and he did not know the right people to **get his foot in the door** somewhere else. So he stayed sous-chef. He still loved the work, he still loved food, but now he spent all day writing menus in his head, **imagining** what **fantastic** and **inventive** food he would serve to people and how much they would love his cooking!

menus - Menü
current job – aktuelle Arbeitsstelle
supportive - unterstützend
make the calls (exp) – andere bestimmen lassen
opening – Freie Stelle (Job)
extremely competitive – extrem konkurrenzfähig
young - jung
experience - erfahren
by comparison (exp) - im Vergleich
get his foot in the door (exp) – den Fuß in die Tür bekommen
imagining - vorstellen
fantastic - fantastisch
inventive - einfallsreich

Tucker started saving **money**, bit by bit, to open his own restaurant. He knew he would never get hired as a chef somewhere else. The only way to do it was to open his own place. He **scrimped** and saved every little bit he could, but at the rate he was going, it would take his whole life to save up enough to open a restaurant! Sous-chefs did not make very much money, after all.

money - Geld
scrimped - knauserte

One day, the head chef brought Tucker into his office. They sat down together, and the chef took off his hat.

"Tucker, I have some news for you."

Tucker held his breath, **fearing**, for a moment, that he was about to get **fired for no good reason**.

"In a couple of **months**, I'll be leaving the restaurant."

"What!" Tucker **exclaimed**. "Why? Is everything okay?"

"Yes, I'm **fine**. Actually, I'm switching careers. I'm tired of food service. I majored in **nutrition** in college, did you know that? I want to be a **nutritionist**. I'm going to get my **certification** and **quit**. I want you to take over for me."

Tucker was **speechless**. He **stared** at the chef in **amazement**.

"**Are you okay**? You don't have to take the job, I just thought I would ask you first, since I thought you wanted it."

"Yes!" Tucker said at last. "I would love to! Thank you chef, thank you so much! It's **literally** a **dream come true**." Tucker sighed with happiness.

Someday a Chef

"Hey, kid, I'm happy for you," the chef **chuckled**. "Have you thought about what kind of **changes** you'll make to the menu?"

"I have!" Tucker exclaimed. "I've thought about it a lot."

"What's the first thing you want to do?" chef asked.

"Well," said Tucker with a smile, "I'm going to make jajangmyeon the house **specialty**!"

fearing - ängstlich
fired - entlassen
for no good reason (exp) – ohne jeglichem Grund
months - Monate
exclaimed - rief
fine – in Ordnung
nutrition - Ernährung
nutritionist - Ernährungsberater
certification - Zertifikat
quit - kündigen
speechless - sprachlos
stared - starren
amazement - Verwunderung
Are you okay (exp) – bist du okay
literally - buchstäblich
dream come true (exp) – ein Traum wird wahr
chuckled - jauchzte
changes - Änderungen
specialty - Spezialität

Vocabulary:

growing up - erwachsen wude
accepted - akzeptieren
reasoned - begründet
sewing - Nähen
writing - Schreiben
sci-fi - Science-Fiction
consequently - folglich
adventurously - sonderlich
fancy - schick
spaghetti - Spaghetti
sauce - Soße
baguette - Baguette
salad - Salat
having company (exp) - Besuch
can - Dose
box - Box
jar - Glas
Frozen pizza - Tiefkühlpizza
household staple – Grundnahrungsmittel im Haushalt
Rarely - Selten
vegetables - Gemüse
window - Fenster
fast food – Fastfood
drive-through (exp) - Durchfahrtsbedienung
hamburgers - Hamburger
appreciated - dankbar
missing - fehlt
culinary wasteland – Kulinarische Einöde
born and raised (exp) - aufgewachsen
exposed - vertraut gemacht
sixth grade – sechste Klasse
sleepovers - Übernachtungen
pizza - Pizza
worried – sorgen machen
refrigerator - Kühlschrank

soda - Limonade
admitted - zugegeben
exclaimed - rief
How else (exp) - wie sonst
conversation - Unterhaltung
ramen – Ramen Nudeln
boiled eggs – gekochte Eier
ddukbokki – Koreanisches Essen
bibimbap – Koreanisches Essen
jajangmyeon – Koreanisches Essen
fried rice – gebratener Reis
kimchi – Koreanisches Essen
jajangmyeon – Koreanisches Essen
gyeongju – Koreanisches Essen
dessert - Nachspeise
embark - einsteigen
magical culinary journey – magische kulinarische Reise
Devote - widmen
energy - Energie
entered - eintreten
packaged - verpackt
cooking shows – Kochsendungen
longing - Sehnsucht
reality - Realität
competed - konkurriert
build - bauen
tallest - höchste
sugar sculpture – Zuckerskulptur
craziest - verrückteste
cake - Kuchen
course - Gang
fastest - schnellste
demonstrates - vorstellt
prepare - vorbereiten
absolutely fascinated – total fasziniert
slicing carrots – Karotten schneiden
thickness - Dicke
texture - Konsistenz

lovingly dice – liebevoll stückeln
onion - Zwiebel
caramelize - Karamellisieren
skillet -Bratpfanne
oil - Öl
dough - Teig
fresh pasta – frische Nudeln
bare hands – blanke Hände
longing - sehnsüchtig
roux - Mehlschwitze
grace - Anmut
ease - Leichtigkeit
breathing - atmen
tender - zart
colors - Farben
delicious - köstlich
was in love (exp) - verliebt
voraciously - heißhungrig
spare -freie
masters -Profis
practice - ausüben
craft - Handwerk
afraid - angst
fire - Feuer
wasted - verschwendet
burnt -verbrannt
distance -Abstand
messed it up (exp) - vermasselt
college - Hochschule
apartment - Wohnung
campus - Universitätsgelände
comfortable - gemütlich
kitchen - Küche
equipped - ausgestattet
brand-new appliances – neue Geräte
sink - Spüle
spacious freezer – geräumige Gefriertruhe
stove - Herd

ceramic glass electric cook top - Cerankochfeld
Finally - endlich
packed - eingepackt
preservatives - Konservierungsstoffe
dish - Gericht
carefully - sorgfältig
ingredients - Zutaten
minced pork – gehacktes Schwein
packet - Packung
noodles - Nudeln
mirin - Reiswein
black bean paste – Schwarze Bohnenpaste
chunjang – Schwarze Bohnenpaste (koreanisch)
carried - beinhalten
in awe - bewundernd
recognize - erinnern
recipe - Rezept
meat - Fleisch
smoke - qualmen
awful - furchtbar
down - runterschalten
crispy - knusprig
closely - genau
accidentally - ausversehen
onion - Zwiebel
zucchini - Zuccini
potato - Kartoffel
radish stayed – Rettich blieb
hard - hart
bean paste – Bohnenpaste
stirred - rührte
bite - Biss
yuck - Pfui
terrible - furchtbar
discouraged - entmutigt
beginner - Anfänger
work your way up (exp) - Hocharbeiten
simply - einfach

resolve - lösen
renewed - erneuern
determined - entschlossen
stir-fry - gebratenes
chicken - Hähnchen
shrimp - Schrimps
tofu - Tofu
snap peas - Erbsen
broccoli - Broccoli
bell peppers - Paprika
dry - trocken
sauce - Soße
weeks - Wochen
experimenting - experimentieren
saute - anbraten
roast - rösten
charcoal grill - Kohlegrill
grill - grillen
cautious - aufmerksam
disrespecting - Nichtachtung
mistakes - Fehler
skill - Fähigkeit
thick - dick
resembled jelly – ähnelt Wackelpudding
salty - salzig
water - Wasser
Dabble - sich versuchen
baking - Backen
admired - bewundern
amazed - begeistert
effort - anstrengung
detail - Detail
pastry chefs – Konditormeister
desserts - Nachtisch
destroyed - vernichtet
calculated - gerechnet
hours - Stunden
portion - Servierung

level - Grad
patience - Geduld
pipe - pumpen
intricate pattern – kompliziertes Muster
royal icing – königliche Zuckerglasur
sugar cookies - Kekse
excellent chocolate cake – hervorragender Schokoladenkuchen
decorations - Dekorationen
buttercream frosting – Buttercreme Glasur
dinner parties – Abendessen
famous - berühmt
potlucks – Essen bei dem jeder etwas mitbringt
obsession - Besessenheit
restaurant - Restaurant
prep cook - Hilfskoch
sliced – in Scheiben geschnitten
chopped - zerhackt
crushed - zerdrückt
was a happy camper (exp) – war glücklich und zufrieden
sous-chef – stellvertretender Küchenchef
called out (exp) - rief
wife - Ehefrau
baby - Baby
chef appointed – Chef ernannte
replacement - Ersatz
to pitch in (exp) - einspringt
absorbing - absorbieren
detail - Detail
operation - Tätigkeit
although - obwohl
nervous - nervös
Orders - Bestellungen
left and right (exp) – links und rechts
barked - bellten
instructing - anweisen
confident - selbstbewussten
tools - Werkzeug

fried - frittiert
sauteed - bratete an
mixed - verrührte
chopped - schnitt
seasoned - würzte
tasted - probierte
flew by (exp) – verging wie im Fluge
afternoon - Nachmittag
midnight - Mitternacht
sworn - geschworen
had such a good time (exp) – so eine gute Zeit
looked up to (exp) – Vorbild (jemanden bewundern)
praised - lobte
respected - respektiert
stepping in - eingesprungen
permanent position – permanente Position
awesome - hervorragend
transfer - versetzen
tirelessly - unermüdlich
business - Themenbereich
with every fiber of his being (exp) – mit jeder Faser seines Körpers
industry - Branche
adored - bewunderte
bustle - Rummel
menus - Menü
current job – aktuelle Arbeitsstelle
supportive - unterstützend
make the calls (exp) – andere bestimmen lassen
opening – Freie Stelle (Job)
extremely competitive – extrem konkurrenzfähig
young - jung
experience - erfahren
by comparison (exp) - im Vergleich
get his foot in the door (exp) – den Fuß in die Tür bekommen
imagining - vorstellen
fantastic - fantastisch
inventive - einfallsreich

fearing - ängstlich
fired - entlassen
for no good reason (exp) – ohne jeglichem Grund
months - Monate
exclaimed - rief
fine – in Ordnung
nutrition - Ernährung
nutritionist - Ernährungsberater
certification - Zertifikat
quit - kündigen
speechless - sprachlos
stared - starren
amazement - Verwunderung
Are you okay (exp) – bist du okay
literally - buchstäblich
dream come true (exp) – ein Traum wird wahr
chuckled - jauchzte
changes - Änderungen
specialty - Spezialität

The Rose Gardener

Thomas was a **gardener**; not just **any old** gardener, but a Master Gardener. He had **studied** hard and learned a lot about **plants** so that he could take the test and earn the **official ltitle** of Master Gardener. He **volunteered** at events all over the **state** of Texas, **educating** children about different areas of gardening like trees and **shrubs**, **flower beds**, and vegetable and **herb** gardens. He **gave lectures** about the **water table**, about **native plants** and **conservation** efforts, about **pollinators** like **bees** and **butterflies**, and anything else someone needed a lecture about! He was invited as a **guest speaker** to classrooms in elementary school and all the way up through college.

Gardener - Gärtner
any old (exp) - gewöhnlicher
studied - studiert
plants - Pflanzen
official title – offizielle Bezeichnung
volunteered - Ehrenamtlich
state - Staat
educating - unterrichten
shrubs - Sträuche
flower beds – Blumenbeete
herb - Kräuter
gave lectures (exp) – hielt Vorträge
water table – Grundwasserspiegel
native plants – einheimische Pflanzen
conservation - Naturschutz
pollinators - Bestäuber
bees - Bienen
butterflies - Schmetterlinge
guest speaker – Gastredner

Outside of his volunteer work, Thomas **spent a lot of time** in his garden. As much time as he could: **one could say** that Thomas was **obsessed** with his garden! He thought about his garden all the time, even when he was away from home. He had been gardening for over forty years, so his garden was very full. He **rarely** got to add new plants, but he liked to **daydream** about new plants all the time. He also like to think about the **existing** plants: how **healthy** and beautiful they were, what different **insects** he had found around them, the **animals** he saw in the **yard**, and how pretty his **lawn** looked when he **mowed** it. Thomas did not care much about the grass. He let **clover** and **Bermuda grass** grow in between the **Fescue** because having a perfect lawn required lots of **harsh chemicals**, **seeding** and re-seeding. Thomas **preferred** to keep his yard as **natural** as he possibly could, so he spent a little extra money for **organic** soil, organic **fertilizers**, organic **seeds**, and organically grown plants (especially **annuals**).

spent a lot of time (exp) – hat viel Zeit verbracht
one could say (exp) – man kann sagen
obsessed - besessen
rarely - kaum
daydream - Tagtraum
existing - existiert
healthy - gesund
insects - Insekten
animals - Tiere
yard - Garten
lawn - Rasen
mowed - gemäht
clover - Klee
Bermuda grass – Bermudagras
Fescue - Schwingelgras
harsh chemicals – strenge Chemikalien
seeding - Platzierungen
preferred - bevorzugen
natural - natürlich
organic - biologisch
fertilizers - Dünger
seeds - Samen
annuals – einjährige Pflanzen

Annuals were Thomas›s **weakness**. He knew that most Master Gardeners, especially ones interested in conservation, did not like annuals because they were usually not native plants and they died very **shortly** after the season ended - but they were so beautiful! They came in so many colors! Deep purple **verbena**, bright **magenta petunias**, and **vibrant** yellow **pansies**; different flowers for every season, which Thomas planted in great big **stone pots** in his front yard. Then, he changed them out every few months.

Annuals – einjährige Pflanzen
weakness - Schwäche
shortly - kurz
verbena - Eisenkraut
magenta petunias – magentafarbige Petunien
vibrant - beschwingte
pansies - Stiefmütterchen
stone pots - Pflanzentöpfe

He had many different types of plants in his yard besides annuals: **perennial** flowers, herbs, trees, and shrubs. Thomas's **pride and joy** were his **rosebushes**. He had over a dozen rosebushes all over his yard, each one a very special **variety**, each one **unique** and **dear** to his heart. There were big roses and small roses, **climbing** roses and shrub roses. There were brilliant white roses, some in a **vivid coral** pink color; classic red roses; and sweet yellow roses with a nice fragrance. Thomas even had a "tree rose," which was not exactly a tree but a shrub rose that had been **pruned** to resemble a tree. The tree rose was in his front yard, near the front porch, so that all the neighbors could see it and **compliment** him on it.

perennial - mehrjährig
pride and joy (exp) – sein ganzer Stolz
rosebushes - Rosensträuche
variety - Vielfalt
unique - einzigartig
dear – teuer (geschätzt)

climbing - klettern
vivid coral – lebhaft korallpink
pruned - kürzen
compliment - ein Kompliment machen

The neighbors always **commented on** Thomas's beautiful garden. Sometimes Thomas felt **lonely**, because he did not have any children and his wife died a long time ago. He did not have family in the **area**, but his neighbors were friendly to him, and he met lots of friends through volunteering as a Master Gardener. Whenever Thomas started to feel lonely, all he had to do was go outside and work in the yard for a **while**. **Eventually**, a neighbor would stop by and **chat** or call to him as they walked by, and even if no one did speak to him while he was outside, Thomas also **considered** the plants his friends. They spoke to him too, in their own special ways. The roses spoke to him most of all.

commented on – sprachen über
lonely - einsam
area - Gegend
while – Weile
Eventually - Letztendlich
chat - unterhalten
considered - ansehen

Thomas loved the roses **almost** like children. He **tended** to them every day: he **weeded**; he **watered**; he pruned; he **fertilized**; and as he gave them the **proper** care, they became more and more beautiful. Which was exactly what Thomas had hoped for, because this year, he was entering his roses in a **competition** at the county fair, and Thomas wanted to win very badly. He'd never won anything in his life, but he thought if he could win, it would be at gardening.

almost - fast
tended - hüten
weeded – jätet
watered - bewässern

fertilized - düngen
proper - korrekt
competition - Wettbewerb

One morning, Thomas anxiously watched the sky, hoping that the **puffy** white **clouds** he saw in the distance might come a little closer and bring some **rain** with them. **Logically**, he knew that they **probably** would not, because rain clouds looked different. Rain clouds were heavy, thick, and dark. When it rained, the clouds covered the whole **entire** sky as far as the eye could see. These clouds were beautiful, bright white, and spaced far apart so that the blue sky showed through between them. The weather today was warm and mild, because it was early summer, and Thomas was getting ready for the competition. He took his morning stroll around the garden at a leisurely pace, pausing to **admire** each **specimen** in his yard, inhaling their **fragrances** and inspecting their **foliage**.

puffy - bauschig
clouds - Wolken
rain - Regen
Logically - Logischerweise
probably - wahrscheinlich
entire - gesamten
admire - bewundern
specimen - Exemplar
fragrances - Düfte
foliage - Blätter

But then, Thomas came upon one of his **prized** roses, the one with coral-colored flowers, and his heart **skipped** a beat when he saw one of the flower buds covered in tiny little green **bugs**.

Aphids. The gardener's **enemy**. Thomas had **fought** aphids before but never right before a competition! Now, he could lose all of his hard work tending to this rose, and if he was not careful, the aphids could **spread** to other plants. They could even take over the whole garden! Thomas began to **panic**, because he did not know what to do. It felt almost **irresponsible** to leave his precious rosebush alone with the aphids **attacking** it, but standing there watching the **infestation** would not help, either! So Thomas made himself leave to go inside and begin consulting his **vast** library of gardening books for help with the aphid **situation**.

prized – geschätzte
skipped - auslassen
bugs - Käfer
Aphids - Blattläuse
enemy - Erzfeind
fought - bekämpft
spread - verteilen
panic - Panik
irresponsible - verantwortungslos
attacking - attakiert
infestation - Verseuchung
vast - riesig
situation - Situation

*"Physical **removal** of the insects may **cure** a small infestation."* said one book.

*"Aphids' natural **predators**, such as **ladybugs** and **nesting** birds, may be **encouraged** or **introduced** to the garden."* advised another.

***Concoct** a tea made from **tobacco** products (finally your uncle's **filthy smoking habit** comes in handy!) and water. Mix this with dish soap and **vinegar** and apply **liberally** to the **affected** plants."* **instructed** a third.

Removal - Entfernen
cure - heilt
predators - Feinde
ladybugs - Marienkäfer
nesting – nisten
encouraged - ermutigt
introduced - vorgestellt

Concoct - zubereiten
tobacco - Tabak
filthy smoking habit – dreckige Rauchangewohnehit
vinegar - Essig
liberally - großzügig
affected - betroffenen
instructed - angeleitet

By the time he had finished reading over all of his gardening **references**, Thomas's head **ached**. **How was he supposed to know** which **remedy** would work? He didn't have time to try them all! He had to know which one was the best. The tobacco and dish soap spray sounded **disgusting** but probably effective, only Thomas didn't know any **smokers**. He was too **afraid** of the bugs coming back to just **pinch** them off the plants. He had read about some **insecticides**, too, but Thomas did not like to use harsh chemicals in his garden.

references - Verweise
ached - schmerzte
How was he supposed to know (exp) – Woher sollte er wissen
remedy - Heilmittel
disgusting - ekelhaft
smokers - Raucher
afraid - Angst
pinch - stibitzen
insecticides - Insektizide

Ultimately, he decided to go buy some ladybugs. He got into his car and drove to the garden center. Although he was **distressed** about the aphids attacking his precious roses, he felt happy, because he loved going to the garden center. He always walked around for at least half an hour to look at all the **exciting** new flowers and trees and to browse the gardening **tools**. Even if he didn't need a tool or **intend** to buy one, it was fun to **look**. Today, however, he only looked for a few minutes, before he approached the **information desk**.

Ultimately - letzendlich
distressed - betrübt
exciting - aufregend
tools - Werkzeuge
intend – vor haben
look - gucken
information desk – Infoschalter

Uh-oh. Thomas stopped about ten **feet** away from the info desk. Thomas **recognized** the person **behind** the **counter** from his gardening club. The old lady (much older, even, than him) did not like Thomas, and she too was going to be in the rose competition! While he knew he might be **acting silly**, Thomas did not trust the lady. What if she told him the wrong thing **on purpose** so that his roses would be **ruined**?

Uh-oh - Ohje
feet - Fuß (Maßeinheit)
recognized - wiedererkannt
behind - hinter
counter - Schalter
acting silly – sich albern verhalten
on purpose – mit Absicht
ruined - ruiniert

"Thomas!" the lady called to him. "What a **pleasant** surprise."

Thomas knew he could not walk away now without being **rude**, so he went over to the information desk and **greeted** her. "Hello, Eugenia. I didn't know you worked here!"

"Yes, you know how much I love gardening. I work here a couple days a week, just helping people with my Master Gardener **knowledge**."

Thomas **squirmed** a little bit. "Yes. **Good for you**, Eugenia. That's very nice."

"So! What brings you to the information desk today?" Eugenia looked a little **smug**. She felt good being the one giving the information, while Thomas was the one who needed help.

Thomas did not want to tell her what his problem was, but he was also not a very good **liar**. He **struggled** to think of something else to say, but then **blurted out**, "One of my roses has aphids, and I want to know the best way to get rid of them in time for the county fair."

"Aphids!" Eugenia cried. "Now that is one garden **pest** I have never been able to **lick** without a lot of insecticide, you know."

pleasant - angenehme
rude - unhöflich
greeted - begrüßt
knowledge -Wissen
squirmed - schauderte
Good for you (exp) – Schön für dich
smug - selbstgefällig
liar - Lügner
struggled – schwer getan
blurted out (exp) – sprach es aus
pest - Plage
lick - lecken

"I don't want to use insecticide," Thomas protested, "that will kill a lot of other insects. I only want to kill the aphids. One of my gardening books said I should buy ladybugs."

"You can certainly try that," Eugenia **sniffed**, "but it has never worked for me." Clearly, Eugenia thought that if it hadn't worked for her, it would not work for anyone.

"I want to try it," Thomas said **firmly**. "Where are the ladybugs?"

"We keep them in a special **holding** area in the back. I'll go get them for you." Eugenia **disappeared** through a door behind the desk. Thomas waited, watching the other **patrons** of the garden center. He almost **forgot** why he was there as he watched a young mother help her tiny son pick out his very own **hand trowel**. Thomas was smiling when Eugenia came back. She set a round **container** on the counter. It was made of hard, clear plastic, so Thomas could see hundreds of tiny little red-and-black ladybugs inside. He smiled again, because he thought ladybugs were **pretty cute**. Eugenia sniffed again, because she thought bugs were pretty **gross**.

sniffed - schnupperte
firmly - ernst
holding - Haltung
disappeared - verschwand
patrons - Gemeinde
forgot - vergessen
hand trowel - Handtuch
container - Behälter
pretty cute – ziemlich niedlich
gross - eklig

"Here you go. Take them to the **register** and pay, they will give you a paper bag and an instruction **booklet**." Eugenia pushed the container toward Thomas.

"Thanks, Eugenia. Have a great day," said Thomas. He picked up the container and went to the register, where his favorite cashier was working. The cashier wished him luck with the aphid problem and tucked the ladybugs into a paper bag, which Thomas **clutched eagerly** as he left, feeling **optimistic** about his purchase.

register - Kasse
booklet - Broschüre
clutched eagerly – packte eifrig
optimistic - optimistisch

When he got back home, Thomas consulted the instruction booklet. *"Spray lady beetles with a fine **mist** of water, as they are usually **dehydrated** when purchased in a garden center."* Thomas felt bad for the dehydrated beetles, so he immediately opened the container, careful not to let any of them out, and sprayed a little water inside.

*"The lady beetles need to be **refrigerated** until immediately before use."* This seemed like a very strange suggestion to Thomas. He felt a little bit guilty putting all of those ladybugs in the refrigerator, but he wanted them to eat the aphids, so he followed instructions.

"Sorry, little guys," he **apologized**, before closing the refrigerator door.

"Release the lady beetles in early evening. If released during the heat of the day, the lady beetles will likely fly away and will not eat the aphids in the desired area." This made sense to Thomas, he **supposed**. Although, he was eager to let the ladybugs out on the rosebush, so it was very hard to wait. He went for a walk, talked to his neighbors, and invited his friend Jim over for dinner. Thomas started preparing a nice meal and, for a while, forgot all about the aphids. He made a **tasty** salad with spinach and chopped **strawberries**. Then he cooked **potatoes** and **steaks** on the **grill** in the back yard. He and Jim sat together on the **patio** to eat, admiring the garden and enjoying the food. By the time dinner was over, it was **dusk**.

mist - Nebel
dehydrated - dehydriert
refrigerated - gekühlt
apologized - entschuldigt
supposed - vermutet
tasty - lecker
strawberries - Erdbeeren
potatoes - Kartoffeln
steaks - Steaks

grill - Grill
patio - Terasse
dusk - Dämmerung

"Time to release the ladybugs!" Thomas **announced**.

"Exciting," said Jim. "I hope they **do the trick**."

"Me too," Thomas agreed. He went inside and took the plastic container out of the refrigerator with **butterflies in his stomach**. He felt **nervous** as he took the precious ladybugs outside and stood before his beloved rosebush.

*"Release the lady beetles towards the bottom of the plant. They will crawl **upwards** in search of aphids."* Thomas crouched down beside the rosebush, tipped the container over one of the bottom branches, and dozens of ladybugs fell out clinging to the branches and leaves. Some of them stuck to the inside of the container, so Thomas reached in and gently pushed them out with his fingertip.

Announced - ankündigen
do the trick (exp) – ich hoffe es klappt
butterflies in his stomach (exp) – Schmetterlinge im Bauch
nervous - nervös
upwards - nach oben

"Now it's just a **waiting game**," he said, standing with arms **akimbo**.

"Sometimes waiting is the hardest thing to do!" Jim said.

"Yes, but **patience** pays off in gardening." Thomas smiled, then turned around to go back to the patio and begin clearing away the dinner dishes.

Three weeks later, the county fair was **in full swing**, and the day of the rose competition had **arrived**. The ladybugs took care of the aphids the same day Thomas put them down, but the blooms never **recovered** from the aphid damage. Thomas had to choose a different rose to enter into the competition, so he chose a shrub with much smaller flowers. The color of the petals was yellow at the base with a bright pink at the edges. It was a very unique-looking flower.

waiting game (exp) - Wartespiel
akimbo – in die Seite gestemmt
patience - Geduld
in full swing (exp) – im vollem Schwung
arrived - angekommen
recovered - erholt

Thomas chose three of the very biggest, **brightest**, most perfect blooms, and cut them off. Cutting the blooms was always **nerve-wracking**, because once they were cut there was nothing else to be done. He put them in a **vase** of cold water and sheltered the blossoms with little plastic bags, securing them to the stems with rubber bands. He drove to the **fairgrounds** where he saw: booths set up as far as the eye could see; a **Ferris wheel** and some other **carnival rides**; and the parking area, which stretched over a dozen **acres** and was packed with hundreds, or maybe even thousands, of cars.

brightest - hellsten
nerve-wracking (exp) – nervenaufraubend
vase - Vase
fairgrounds - Jahrmarkt
Ferris wheel - Riesenrad
carnival rides – Jahrmarkt
acres – weite Flächen

As he **wandered** through the fair with his prized roses clutched to his chest, Thomas **grinned hugely**. Children **screamed** with **delight** on the **roller coaster**. **Funnel cakes frying** smelled so **delicious**, and the **cotton candy** smelled so sweet. Young boys played games of **skill** to try to win a **prize** for their girlfriends. Away from the games and rides, people sold **handicrafts** and

artwork. There was even a booth where kids could get their faces painted to look like a **tiger**, a **shark** or any other animal **imaginable**. Thomas had not been to the county fair in so many years that he had forgotten what fun it was! He was so **delighted** by the **sights**, **sounds**, and **smells**, that by the time he reached the **exhibition** tent, his nerves were gone.

wandered – schlenderte
grinned hugely -großes Grinsen
screamed - schreiten
delight -Freude
roller coaster - Achterbahn
Funnel cakes – Trichterkuchen
frying - frittiert
delicious - köstlich
cotton candy - Zuckerwatte
skill - Fähigkeiten
prize - Preise
handicrafts - handgemachtes
artwork - Kunst
tiger -Tiger
shark - Hai
imaginable - vorstellbar
delighted - erfreut
sights - Anblick
sounds - Geräusche
smells - Gerüche
exhibition - Ausstellung

A dozen tables sat in rows inside the tent. Most of them were **empty** right now because Thomas was a little bit **early**. He looked at his **registration** number, then he started wandering among the tables looking for his **designated spot**.

"Hello, Thomas!" Eugenia said. She was already set up and standing **proudly** beside her **classic** red long-**stem** rose.

"Hi, Eugenia," Thomas said. He saw his number on the table

right **beside** her. He **sighed** a little, then went over and started setting up his blooms.

empty - leer
early - früh
registration - Registrierung
designated spot – zugeteilten Platz
proudly - stolz
classic - klassisch
stem - Stängel
beside - neben
sighed - seufzte

People **gradually** began filling the tent. Thomas watched them, in **awe** of the **sheer** variety of roses that came through the tent. Every size and color imaginable, and so many different shapes! Some of them had a **single layer** of petals, some of them were **double** layered, and some of them were **practically bursting** with petals! It was **amazing**! But Thomas did not see any other blooms like his own. He was the only person with a two-color rose, and his **tender** care of the roses had resulted in the most perfect blooms in the tent.

A while later, the **judging commenced** and when it was over, they pinned the **first-place meda**l on Thomas's aphid-free rose.

gradually -allmählich
awe - Ehrfurcht
sheer - schiere
single layer – einzelne Schicht
double - doppelt
practically bursting – praktisch platzend
amazing - wundervoll
tender - liebevoll
judging commenced – Beurteilung beginnt
first-place medal – Medaille für den ersten Platz

Vocabulary:

Gardener - Gärtner
any old (exp) - gewöhnlicher
studied - studiert
plants - Pflanzen
official title – offizielle Bezeichnung
volunteered - Ehrenamtlich
state - Staat
educating - unterrichten
shrubs - Sträuche
flower beds – Blumenbeete
herb - Kräuter
gave lectures (exp) – hielt Vorträge
water table – Grundwasserspiegel
native plants – einheimische Pflanzen
conservation - Naturschutz
pollinators - Bestäuber
bees - Bienen
butterflies - Schmetterlinge
guest speaker – Gastredner
spent a lot of time (exp) – hat viel Zeit verbracht
one could say (exp) – man kann sagen
obsessed - besessen
rarely - kaum
daydream - Tagtraum
existing - existiert
healthy - gesund
insects - Insekten
animals - Tiere
yard - Garten
lawn - Rasen
mowed - gemäht
clover - Klee
Bermuda grass – Bermudagras
Fescue - Schwingelgras
harsh chemicals – strenge Chemikalien

seeding - Platzierungen
preferred - bevorzugen
natural - natürlich
organic - biologisch
fertilizers - Dünger
seeds - Samen
annuals – einjährige Pflanzen
Annuals – einjährige Pflanzen
weakness - Schwäche
shortly - kurz
verbena - Eisenkraut
magenta petunias – magentafarbige Petunien
vibrant - beschwingte
pansies - Stiefmütterchen
stone pots - Pflanzentöpfe
perennial - mehrjährig
pride and joy (exp) – sein ganzer Stolz
rosebushes - Rosensträuche
variety - Vielfalt
unique - einzigartig
dear – teuer (geschätzt)
climbing - klettern
vivid coral – lebhaft korallpink
pruned - kürzen
compliment - ein Kompliment machen
commented on – sprachen über
lonely - einsam
area - Gegend
while – Weile
Eventually - Letztendlich
chat - unterhalten
considered - ansehen
almost - fast
tended - hüten
weeded – jätet
watered - bewässern
fertilized - düngen
proper - korrekt

competition - Wettbewerb
puffy - bauschig
clouds - Wolken
rain - Regen
Logically - Logischerweise
probably - wahrscheinlich
entire - gesamten
admire - bewundern
specimen - Exemplar
fragrances - Düfte
foliage - Blätter
prized – geschätzte
skipped - auslassen
bugs - Käfer
Aphids - Blattläuse
enemy - Erzfeind
fought - bekämpft
spread - verteilen
panic - Panik
irresponsible - verantwortungslos
attacking - attakiert
infestation - Verseuchung
vast - riesig
situation - Situation
Removal - Entfernen
cure - heilt
predators - Feinde
ladybugs - Marienkäfer
nesting – nisten
encouraged - ermutigt
introduced - vorgestellt
Concoct - zubereiten
tobacco - Tabak
filthy smoking habit – dreckige Rauchangewohnehit
vinegar - Essig
liberally - großzügig
affected - betroffenen
instructed - angeleitet

references - Verweise
ached - schmerzte
How was he supposed to know (exp) – Woher sollte er wissen
remedy - Heilmittel
disgusting - ekelhaft
smokers - Raucher
afraid - Angst
pinch - stibitzen
insecticides - Insektizide
Ultimately - letzendlich
distressed - betrübt
exciting - aufregend
tools - Werkzeuge
intend – vor haben
look - gucken
information desk – Infoschalter
Uh-oh - Ohje
feet - Fuß (Maßeinheit)
recognized - wiedererkannt
behind - hinter
counter - Schalter
acting silly – sich albern verhalten
on purpose – mit Absicht
ruined - ruiniert
pleasant - angenehme
rude - unhöflich
greeted - begrüßt
knowledge -Wissen
squirmed - schauderte
Good for you (exp) – Schön für dich
smug - selbstgefällig
liar - Lügner
struggled – schwer getan
blurted out (exp) – sprach es aus
pest - Plage
lick - lecken
sniffed - schnupperte
firmly - ernst

holding - Haltung
disappeared - verschwand
patrons - Gemeinde
forgot - vergessen
hand trowel - Handtuch
container - Behälter
pretty cute – ziemlich niedlich
gross - eklig
register - Kasse
booklet - Broschüre
clutched eagerly – packte eifrig
optimistic - optimistisch
mist - Nebel
dehydrated - dehydriert
refrigerated - gekühlt
apologized - entschuldigt
supposed - vermutet
tasty - lecker
strawberries - Erdbeeren
potatoes - Kartoffeln
steaks - Steaks
grill - Grill
patio - Terasse
dusk - Dämmerung
Announced - ankündigen
do the trick (exp) – ich hoffe es klappt
butterflies in his stomach (exp) – Schmetterlinge im Bauch
nervous - nervös
upwards - nach oben
waiting game (exp) - Wartespiel
akimbo – in die Seite gestemmt
patience - Geduld
in full swing (exp) – im vollem Schwung
arrived - angekommen
recovered - erholt
brightest - hellsten
nerve-wracking (exp) – nervenaufraubend
vase - Vase

fairgrounds - Jahrmarkt
Ferris wheel - Riesenrad
carnival rides – Jahrmarkt
acres – weite Flächen
wandered – schlenderte
grinned hugely -großes Grinsen
screamed - schreiten
delight -Freude
roller coaster - Achterbahn
Funnel cakes – Trichterkuchen
frying - frittiert
delicious - köstlich
cotton candy - Zuckerwatte
skill - Fähigkeiten
prize - Preise
handicrafts - handgemachtes
artwork - Kunst
tiger -Tiger
shark - Hai
imaginable - vorstellbar
delighted - erfreut
sights - Anblick
sounds - Geräusche
smells - Gerüche
exhibition - Ausstellung
empty - leer
early - früh
registration - Registrierung
designated spot – zugeteilten Platz
proudly - stolz
classic - klassisch
stem - Stängel
beside - neben
sighed - seufzte
gradually -allmählich
awe - Ehrfurcht
sheer - schiere
single layer – einzelne Schicht

double - doppelt
practically bursting – praktisch platzend
amazing - wundervoll
tender - liebevoll
judging commenced – Beurteilung beginnt
first-place medal – Medaille für den ersten Platz

Rückschluss

"One language sets you in a corridor for life.
Two languages open every door along the way."
Frank Smith

Eine zweite Sprache kann Türen öffnen, von denen du niemals gedacht hättest, dass sie existieren, oder nie daran gedacht hättest den Schritt in die Richtung zu wagen. Ich hoffe, dass das Buch dir damit geholfen hat. Viel Anstrengung steckt hinter diesem Buch und dessen Veröffentlichung. Zu wissen, dass ich geholfen habe den Weg für dich zu pflastern, um eine neue Sprache zu lernen – und sicher zu gehen, dass du Spaß dabei hast - macht es die Anstrengung wert.

Nachdem du das Buch gelesen hast, solltest du schon Fortschritte gemacht haben. Du hast hunderte nutzvolle neue englische Wörter und Redewendungen in deinem Vokabular aufgenommen und dein Selbstbewusstsein im Lesen und Schreiben wird sich auch verstärken. All jenes, mit Außnahme von der Aussprache und Hörübungen, werden unterstüzt von dem dazu gehörigen Hörbuch.

Falls dir dieses Buch geholfen hat, unterstütze es bitte und schreibe mir eine ehrliche Meinung. Deine Bewertung ist sehr geschätzt und wir sind sehr dankbar dafür.

Vielen Dank.

Jack

Anleitung zur Nutzung der Audio-Datei

Du hast sicherlich bemerkt, dass die Links zu den Audio-Dateien direkt in den Geschichten der E-Books angegeben sind. Dies wird dir den Zugang zu den MP3-Dateien um ein vielfaches erleichtern. Für iPadnutzer und Nutzer ohne Dropbox gibt es allerdings zusätzliche Anleitungen:

Link zum Download der MP3-Datei :
http://myenglishroutine.com/download-learn-english-stories/

Dieses Produkt ist vollständig kompatibel mit allen iOS Geräten, doch auf Grund der begrenzten Steuerung des Dateisystems in Apple Geräten, musst du zu Beginn die Dateien auf deinen PC herunterladen. Hier sind die Schritte aufgelistet.

1. Download auf den PC

- Nutze entweder den Download-Link aus der E-Mail der Kaufsbestätigung, oder mit deinem Nutzerkonto und lade die -zip Datei auf deinen PC.

- Beachte: diese Dateien können groß sein, versuche also nicht die .zip Datei zu öffnen, bis dir dein Browser mitteilt, dass die Datei vollständig heruntergeladen wurde (normalerweise in einigen Minuten bei einer Breitbandverbindung, doch wenn deine Verbindung unzuverlässig ist, könnte es 10 bis 20 Minuten in Anspruch nehmen).

2. Entpacke die .zip Datei

- Sollte dein Computer auf automatische Entpackung von .zip Dateien eingestellt sein, wirst du einen Ordner in deinem Downloads-Ordner vorfinden. Mache ansonsten einen Doppelklick auf die .zip Datei, um die Datei automatisch in einen Ordner mit den MP3- und PDF Dateien zu entpacken.

3. Importiere die Datei in iTunes

- In iTunes, wähle die Datei > In Bibliothek hinzufügen Menüpunkt. Navigiere zum Ordner, wo sich der XXXXXX Ordner befindet und wähle alle MP3-Dateien aus. Klicke auf Öffnen.

- Sollte dein iTunes auf den Voreinstellungen eingetellt sein, wird es die gesamten My English Routine MP3-Dateien in die iTunes Medienbibliothek kopieren. (Um sicherzugehen, dass die Dateien in deine eigene Sammlung kopiert werden, gehe auf iTunes > Bevorzugung° und klicke auf den «Erweitert» Tab. Diesen solltest du unten sehen können.)

4. Synchronisiere dein iPad/iPhone mit iTunes/iCloud

- Die gesamten Audiodateien sollten nun im Learn English Artist auftauchen.

Alternativ:

- Du kannst dir dieses Video anschauen: https://www.youtube.com/watch?v=a_1VDD9KJhc?

- Du kannst die ersten eine Minute und 20 Sekunden der Erklärung überspringen.

Solltest du immer noch Probleme vorfinden, bitte schreib mir an folgende E-Mail: contact@myenglishroutine.com

Mit all dem gesagt, möchte ich dir herzlichst für den Kauf dieses Buches danken und hoffe, dass du mit diesen Geschichten eine wundervolle Zeit beim Lernen haben wirst.

Vielen Dank.

Probleme beim downloaden der MP3-Datei ?
Wende dich an Fred unter contact@myenglishroutine.com
Vielen lieben Dank.

Printed in Poland
by Amazon Fulfillment
Poland Sp. z o.o., Wrocław

57350554R00087